D. & company Appleton

New York illustrated

a pictorial delineation of street scenes, buildings, river views, and other features of

the great metropolis

D. & company Appleton

New York illustrated
a pictorial delineation of street scenes, buildings, river views, and other features of the great metropolis

ISBN/EAN: 9783337377427

Printed in Europe, USA, Canada, Australia, Japan

Cover: Foto ©Andreas Hilbeck / pixelio.de

More available books at **www.hansebooks.com**

A PICTORIAL DELINEATION OF STREET SCENES, BUILDINGS, RIVER VIEWS, AND OTHER FEATURES OF THE GREAT METROPOLIS.

"LIBERTY ENLIGHTENING THE WORLD."

BY BARTHOLDI.

(To be erected on Bedloe's Island, in the harbor.)

NEW YORK:

D. APPLETON & COMPANY, PUBLISHERS,

1, 3, & 5 BOND STREET.

1881.

CONTENTS.

LIST OF ENGRAVINGS.

NEW YORK ILLUSTRATED.

THE SITUATION.

New York from Fort Wadsworth, Staten Island.

WHAT Boswell said of London is scarcely less true of New York. Its aspects are manifold, and, while each man finds in it the Mecca of his pursuits, it comprehends not one class alone, but the whole of human life in all its variety. The city of New York now includes Manhattan Island; Blackwell's, Ward's, and Randall's Islands in the East River; Governor's, Bedloe's, and Ellis's Islands in the bay, occupied by the United States Government; and a portion of the mainland north of Manhattan Island, separated from it by Harlem River and Spuyten Duyvil Creek. It is bounded north by the city of Yonkers, east by the Bronx and the East River, south by the bay, and west by the Hudson River. Its extreme length north from the Battery is sixteen miles; its greatest width from the mouth of the Bronx west to the Hudson is four and a half miles. Its area is forty-one and a half square miles, or twenty-six thousand acres.

Manhattan Island, upon which the city is mainly built, is about thirteen and a half miles in length on one side and eight on the other, is one mile and three fifths broad on an average, and is bounded at its northern extremity by the Harlem River, which, with Spuyten Duyvil Creek, connects the Hudson River and East River. It is surrounded by water navigable for the most part by the largest vessels, and its harbor is one of the safest, largest, and most beautiful in the world.

Less than three centuries have elapsed since Henry Hudson, the Dutch navigator, passed through the Narrows and disembarked from his little schooner on the present site of the Battery.

Traders followed Hudson, and in 1614 the future metropolis of the New World consisted of a small fort on the site of Bowling Green, and four houses. It was then called "Nieu Amsterdam," and the domain acquired was named the New Netherlands.

When it finally came into possession of the English in 1674, and the name was changed to New York, the settlement expanded and grew with great rapidity. The spirit of the staid and conservative Dutch burgher gave way to that of the pushing and energetic Anglo-Saxon, a race distinguished in history for its success in colonization, and the union of progress and stability which it stamps on its institutions, both political and social.

In 1699 the population had increased to about 6,000. At the beginning of the nineteenth century the number had reached 60,000, and the city extended about two miles north from the Battery; in 1830 it was 202,000; in 1850, 515,000; in 1860, 805,000; in 1870, 942,000; and in 1880, according to census reports recently published, a trifle over 1,250,000. Until the latter part of

New York from the Hudson.

1873 it ended at the Harlem River, but in the November elections of that year the towns of West Farms, Morrisania, and Kings Bridge, hitherto a part of Westchester County, were annexed to the advancing metropolis.

Perhaps no harbor in the world is more picturesque, with the exception of the Bay of Naples, than that of New York. From some elevated point on Staten Island the observer may gaze on a vista of natural beauty, heightened by suggestions of human interest and activity, which alike charms the eye and stirs the imagination. The outer bar is at Sandy Hook, eighteen miles from the Battery, and is crossed by two ship-channels from twenty-one to thirty-two feet deep at ebb-tide, and from twenty-seven to thirty-nine feet at the flood, thus admitting ships of the greatest draught. The Narrows is the name of the strait by which the inner bay communicates with the outer or maritime bay, and is formed by the approach of the shores of Long Island and Staten Island within a mile of each other. This strait may be likened to a gateway from the ocean, while standing like huge sentinels to guard the watery pass are Forts Wadsworth (formerly called Richmond) and

Tompkins on the verge of the Staten Island shore, and Fort Hamilton on the Long Island shore.

From the parapet of Fort Wadsworth the beauty of the panorama unfolds itself in a picture of surpassing charm. In the far distance gleam the innumerable spires of the city, dwarfed into a multitude of glittering points, and the bright waters of the bay toss a multitude of vessels of all descriptions, from tiny tugs and sail-boats to huge three-masters and ocean-steamships arriving and departing. In one direction the eye takes in the green sweep of Long Island, built down to the very water's edge with trimly-kept villas; in another, a haze vaguely reveals the cities of Jersey City and Hoboken, lying across the Hudson from New York. On a pleasant day the brilliancy of the American atmosphere makes this vision of shining waters, white sails, distant spires, and green bluffs, highly fascinating.

As the inward-bound traveler sails fairly within the bay, the picture becomes more and more striking. He is now within the heart of a fleet of stately ships and steamers, plowing a surface that has been cut by all the keels of the civilized world. In the foreground there are patches of green that in the summer sun sparkle like great emeralds in a silver setting—Bedloe's, Ellis's, and Governor's Islands, whereon are defensive fortifications, Bedloe's Island being the proposed site of the colossal statue of Liberty, the gift of the French people, now being sculptured by Bartholdy. The traveler looks on a map every item of which is eloquent with busy life.

In front looms the great metropolis, with its miles of roofs and broken outlines of spires, towers, and domes, now sharply cut to the perception, and telling of religion, thought, art, trade, and industry, developed under their busiest conditions. On either side, as far as the eye can reach, the water-line is fringed with a dense forest of

Lower Part of the City of New York, from the Bay

masts, from which fly the vari-colored flags that represent the commerce of the globe, and suggest such a wonderful story of international relationship, the brotherhood of man. On the left we see the cities tributary to New York which nestle on the New Jersey shore; on the right, Brooklyn, the "City of Churches," the large dormitory of New York's surplus population. Spanning the East River, as that strait is called which connects Long Island Sound with the bay of New York, in one bold leap from shore to shore, the colossal structure of the Brooklyn Bridge, nearly sixteen hundred feet long, and the largest structure of its kind in the world, greets the eye. The water is black with ferry-boats and small steamboats, and the intense vitality and movement of the scene can hardly be described in adequate words.

The situation of New York for commercial purposes is not surpassed. Lying between the North—or, more properly speaking, Hudson—and the East Rivers, it has two very extended and convenient water-fronts, making a total length of dock-line not equaled by that of any city of its size in the world. The water-fronts of Brooklyn, Jersey City, and Hoboken belong

View of New York from Brooklyn Heights.

too, in every essential sense, to New York, and represent its shipping interests. The Hudson River, which flows on the west side of the city, bears an enormous aggregate of freight and passenger-travel, and offers to the stranger one of the most picturesque journeys in the world, not excepting even the traditional attractions of the river Rhine. Within eyeshot indeed of the city, the lofty Palisades rise boldly picturesque, and wooded to their very tops, while glimpses of handsome villas and towns can be caught in the distance.

On the east side of the city the Sound pours its waters through a narrow gateway, and serves a valuable commercial use in giving easy water-carriage between the metropolis and the New England coast. Until within a recent period the East River passage was made somewhat dangerous by the submarine rocks and reefs of Hell Gate, as a portion of the strait is called; but these hidden obstacles to free navigation have now been so far destroyed as to make the passage perfectly safe and easy.

In the East River lie three striking islands—Blackwell's, Randall's, and Ward's—which give great variety to the scene, and are occupied by punitive and charitable institutions, while beyond these the shores of Long Island and New York slope away to a greater distance from each other, showing a succession of charming country-seats and beautiful wooded reaches as far as the eye can extend, which seems merely an extension of the city, gradually dissolving into green and cultivated fields and pleasure-seats.

Such is the situation of the city of New York, the third great capital of the world, and destined ultimately, perhaps, to be its first—a city unrivaled in situation, and in all those facilities and advantages which make a great center of civilization.

STREET SCENES.

THE stranger visiting New York is at once impressed by the intense activity and bustle alike visible and audible in all the conditions of its street-life. The crush of carriages, drays, trucks, and other vehicles, private and public, roaring and rattling over the stone-paved streets; the crowds of swiftly-moving men walking as if not to lose a second of time, their faces preoccupied and eager; the sidewalks encumbered, without regard to the convenience of pedestrians, with boxes and bales of goods—in a word, the whole aspect of New York in its business portions is a true key to the character of its population, as the most energetic and restless of people.

The Battery, which looks out on the noble bay, is comparatively a serene and restful oasis in the fierce turmoil of city life, but one hardly crosses its boundaries without feeling the feverish heart-beat of the metropolis. Walking up Broadway only a few squares, we quickly find

Wall Street, with Treasury Building at the right, and Trinity Church at the head of the Street.

Drexel Building, corner of Broad and Wall Streets, and Stock Exchange.

ourselves in that network of thoroughfares which lies around Wall Street, a financial center, only second to Lombard Street, London, in the variety and weight of its international interests.

At the head of Wall Street, on Broadway, Trinity Church uplifts its graceful spire as if a perpetual reminder of more solemn things; but the busy money-getters, who swarm like flies under the shadow of its venerable walls, find no time or taste to linger over such reflections. The congeries of streets running parallel with Wall Street for two or three squares, and crossing it, are lined with massive and splendid structures, in which the principal banking and railway business of the continent is transacted. Wall Street proper is about half a mile long, extending from Broadway to the East River, and in it are the Stock Exchange, the Sub-Treasury, and the Custom-House. The street derives its name from the fact that in the old Dutch days the city wall ran along this limit, the land to the north being common pasturage. In the building which stood on the site of the present Sub-Treasury,

the first Congress of the United States after the adoption of the Constitution assembled, and under its portico George Washington was inaugurated first President. The fine structure which now lifts its front of marble on the site is two hundred and eighty feet long, eighty feet wide, and eighty feet high. The main entrance is in Wall Street, and is made by an imposing flight of eighteen broad marble steps.

At the corner of Broad and Wall Streets we find the Drexel Building, occupied by Drexel, Morgan & Co., the bankers, and the Leather Manufacturers' National Bank. It is six stories high, built of white marble in the Renaissance style. Within the walls it is two hundred and two by seventy-five feet. Its erection cost seven hundred thousand dollars. The tall marble building seen on the right of the structure is the Stock Exchange, which is in Broad Street, near Wall, with two other entrances on Wall and New Streets. The offices of the brokers who live, move, and have their being in this atmosphere of speculation, and manipulate by far the greater portion of the stocks, bonds, and money of the country, occupy nearly every building for several squares around this financial center. The throng is great and continuous, and on a great field day in the stock-market the excitement almost reaches delirium, presenting to the unsuspicious stranger almost the aspect of an out-door bedlam.

Bank-messengers with actual bags of gold and packages of bonds easily convertible into gold; office-boys with saucy manners and no less saucy faces; shrewd detectives with quiet, unobtrusive ways, altogether unsuspicious; telegraph-boys, in neat uniforms, carrying yellow envelopes, that contain words penned only a few minutes before in London, Paris, or San Francisco; railway magnates more important in swaying the solid destinies of the world than many kings; spruce clerks and laborious porters —all these and other elements are included in the great tide of life.

Amid all the turmoil the chimes of Old Trinity burst into the strong melody of a hymn, and ring out the promises of the Eternal Rock in tones that the uproar of traffic can not drown. The grand old church in this confusion of commerce, embodying in its Gothic architecture centuries of suffering and victory, pathetically appeals to the veneration of the passer-by, but those absorbed in the worship of Mammon scarcely cast a glance at the historic sanctuary.

Let us step for a moment from the life of the streets into the human din of the Stock Exchange. The interior is occupied by a spacious and lofty hall, having a gallery across one end for visitors. When business is at its height, the scene is a strange one. The visitor looks down on a tangled mass of human beings, shrieking

Nassau Street, north from Wall Street.

and waving their arms aloft like madmen. No order or purpose would seem to reign in this confusion, but underneath and behind all this apparent chaos run the most intelligent plans and purposes, and a system which is like a piece of clock-work. The stranger visiting New York finds no more interesting spectacle than the interior of the Stock Exchange during a time of very active speculation.

Looking northward from the Treasury we have a view of Nassau Street—a wonderfully busy thoroughfare, crowded near its lower portion with several very stately bank-buildings, the Bank of Commerce, the Continental Bank, and the Fourth National among them, with several handsome structures occupied by a number of the great private banking-houses, the well-known Brown Brothers being among them. On the

Pine Street.

right, two squares distant, is the time-honored church until recently occupied as a post-office, with its moldy and time-stained walls, telling with grave fidelity of an ancient and varied history. In early times it was known as the Middle Dutch Church, and during the Revolution was used as a riding-school for the British cavalry, and a military prison wherein hundreds of American captives were huddled and died. Its uses as a post-office terminated in September of

1875, and it is now divided into various retail stores.

A walk down Wall Street will well repay the visitor, for he will see not a few of the handsomest banking institutions in America, and a display of noble architecture such as is not presented in the same compass elsewhere on this continent. Chief among these is the handsome structure known as the Bank of New York; and the once famous Merchants' Exchange, now the Custom-House, the latter being a model of solidity and graceful proportions. A little farther down Wall, we cross Pearl Street, the locality of cotton-brokers, the Cotton Exchange, and wholesale houses in various merchandise. At the foot of Wall Street is one of the ferries which connect New York with Brooklyn.

Proceeding one square northward, we find ourselves in Pine Street, a finely-built thoroughfare on which there are many noble and massive structures occupied by banks and other corporate companies, but rather somber from its narrowness and the lofty buildings which keep it in shadow. At the head of the street stands the Martyrs' Monument in Trinity churchyard.

Nassau Street, also quite narrow, is for the most part handsomely built, and a street of much importance, as, apart from a great variety of business transacted there, it is one of the principal radii of Wall Street. Its northern terminus is Printing-House Square, opposite City Hall Park. Portions of Nassau Street are peculiarly notable for its second-hand book - shops and stalls, and buyers from all portions of the country gather at these antiquarian resorts to pick up old editions not easily obtainable elsewhere. Our illustration gives a view of the upper part of the street. The massive structure to the right is the Morse Building, at the corner of Beekman Street, a great colony of many offices, looming up to a vast height. Beyond may be seen the tower of the Tribune Building, facing Printing-House Square.

Few of the down-town streets offer more interest and variety to the eye of the stranger than Fulton Street, which extends from river to river, having at its termini two of the most important markets in the city, Washington Market on the North River, and Fulton Market at the East River terminus. It is the principal approach to Fulton Ferry, which is the most largely patronized of the New York ferries, and which in the morning from seven to ten, and in the evening from four to seven, presents a most animated scene of diversified throngs moving to

Upper part of Nassau Street.

and fro from Brooklyn. At the busiest times of these hours the boats are so packed with human beings that there is scarcely standing-room for another passenger.

The street itself is a scene of much animation and movement. It is lined with small retail shops for the most part, but shops of the better description, in the part nearer the ferry; while adjacent Broadway it contains large wholesale warehouses. Probably nowhere in New York is a greater variety of articles offered for sale, from pins and needles to heavy iron-work, from guns and fishing-tackle to the costliest jewelry, from books and stationery to every article of wearing-apparel, from paintings and bric-à-brac to old junk-iron. The irregular line of this thoroughfare presents a constant throng of pedestrians, and, as it is the main route from Brooklyn, nowhere off Broadway can be seen a larger number of well-dressed men and women in down-town New York.

Fulton Market for many years has been one of the celebrated places of New York to which most strangers are desirous of paying a visit. The buildings themselves are now very old, and have long been felt to be entirely inadequate to their purpose, but all attempts to have them removed and new buildings erected have thus far failed. Fulton Market has two specialties—fish, which are sold on the northern or Beekman Street side of the building; and oysters, which are served in all styles on the southern and eastern sides—Dorlon's place having among the oyster-shops a reputation which is known far and wide.

Two squares above the ferry, Fulton Street is crossed by the New York Elevated Railway, and a station exists at the corner. The difficulties of utilizing narrow streets for the necessities of the elevated roads are very well exemplified in this case. It was found necessary to transform a portion of the old United States Hotel (in the early part of this century one of the most aristocratic and exclusive places of its kind in the city) into a railway-station, as the street space did not admit of such a use. The omnibus and street-car lines which run on Fulton Street, the throngs of trucks and drays, the mass of pedestrians, and the pictorial variety of the shops, combine to make the ensemble a very amusing one.

Northward of Fulton Street and extending from City Hall Park to the East River, the explorer finds himself in the so-called "Swamp," which is the center of the hide and leather trade of New York. The name was given on account of the low situation, which caused it to be over-

flowed at very high tides. The streets in this region are short and narrow, and the air is strongly impregnated with, the pungent odor of salted hides and fresh sole-leather, mixed with the more aromatic smell of kid, morocco, and calf-skin. This business portion of New York still supplies most of the country with the articles in which it deals, though, since so many other ports of entry have been established throughout the country, the amount of the trade has somewhat fallen off. The approaches of the East River Bridge skirt the Swamp on the north, and a wide thoroughfare is replacing Frankfort Street, which runs parallel with these approaches.

The solidity and massiveness of the great stone arches which span the streets at the approach of the East River Bridge give perhaps a more vivid realization of the enterprise than the full view of the bridge from the river, for here the sense of proportion, mingled with the effects of sky and water, lessens the conception of bigness in detail. A full description of the bridge will be found elsewhere.

Returning now to Broadway, let us take a stand on the Post-Office corner at the junction of Broadway and Park Row and look at the animated scene, than which nothing in the street-life of New York is more striking. From morning till night there moves by an ever-changing procession of vehicles that have poured into the great artery from a thousand tributaries, and, to cross Broadway at times at this spot, one must needs be a sort of animated billiard-ball, with power to carom from wheel to wheel, until he can safely "pocket" his personal corporosity on the opposite walk. The crush of vehicles here is sometimes so great as to delay movement for ten minutes or more, and it requires the greatest energy on the part of the police to disentangle the dense, chaotic mass and set it in progress again. For those who are not obliged to cross the choked-up thoroughfare, the scene is full of a brief amusement—hack-drivers, truckmen, omnibus-drivers, swearing vehemently at each other or interchanging all kinds of "chaff"; passengers indignantly railing at the delay, and police-officers yelling and waving their clubs in their attempts to get the machinery of travel again running smoothly. If at such a time a fire-engine comes rattling up the street posthaste for the scene of a fire, and attempts to enforce its right of way, the confusion becomes doubly confounded, and the scene a veritable pandemonium. Ordinarily, however, such tangles of traffic do not occur, for this locality is fully supplied with policemen, whose main busi-

Fulton Street, looking toward Brooklyn Ferry.

ness it is to facilitate the passage of travel and prevent such a blockade as we have described.

The outlook down Broadway from the Post-Office is in all respects picturesque and impressive, and fills the mind with a vivid sense of the immense activity of New York life. In the distance the towers of Trinity Church and the Equitable Life Insurance Building lift themselves as landmarks, and noble buildings thickly stud the squares between. The New York Evening Post Building and the Western Union Telegraph Building catch the eye for their massiveness and dignity; and directly opposite the spectator, but standing diagonally to each other, the Astor House and Herald Building demand the attention as representing institutions which have been household words in New York for the last forty years or more. Up and down this vista roars and streams an ocean-tide of travel and traffic, and the eye can find food for continual interest in its changing kaleidoscope. Well-dressed men and women are brushed in the throng by beggars and laborers grimed with the dust of work; and grotesquely-attired negroes, with huge advertising placards strapped to the front and back, pace up and down, in happy ignorance of the inconvenience they give to others by taking up a double share of room. Fruit and flower stands offer their tempting burdens on every corner, and retail venders of all kinds peddle their goods, and add fresh discord to the din by their shrill crying of their wares. About six o'clock in the afternoon, however, the feverish activity of this region begins to abate, and it is not long before the appearance of the scene becomes lethargic and quiet. Down-town New York has now begun to go to sleep, and it will not be many hours before the silence and emptiness will be alone relieved by the blaze of lights in the newspaper establishments of Printing-House Square and the Western Union Telegraph Building, by the occasional tramp of the policeman or reporter, or the rattling of a casual carriage over the stony pave. This busy part of the city will not begin to waken again till about five o'clock in the morning, when the numerous street-car lines which terminate in this vicinity commence to run their cars, bringing down porters, mechanics, and laborers, as the vanguard of the great army whose thronging battalions will make the new day the repetition of the one before.

From Chambers Street, the northern boundary of the City Hall Park, to Fourteenth Street, Broadway presents to the eye a picture of active business-life in all the departments of trade, except the more heavy and crude articles of mer-

chandise, such as iron, hardware, food-products, etc., which have their headquarters in the lower streets. Every square is massively built with imposing structures devoted to dealers in the textile fabrics and fancy-goods, and the signs of manufacturers of clothing, boots and shoes, etc., are seen on every side. During the busy seasons of the year the sidewalks are so encumbered with boxes and bales that passage is difficult for the pedestrian, and the great warehouses are ablaze with lights nearly all night to accommodate the pressure of business, which taxes the utmost efforts of the merchant and his clerks. Nearly all the wholesale trade of New York, in the lines indicated above, is concentrated on this section of Broadway and several side squares either way from the central thoroughfare.

At Canal Street, which was once the bed of a rivulet, the view up and down Broadway is exceedingly brilliant and picturesque. As far as the eye can reach it gathers in a range of business palaces, representing every variety of taste, style, and beauty, while between them and on the sidewalk is an ever-changing scene in which light, color, and motion, combine to create a charm that never tires. There is a fascination even in the throng of vehicles, the faces in the omnibuses and private carriages, the gay turnouts and handsome equipages; and in the strange commingling of people passing to and fro, representing every State and country, every style of dress from that of the Oriental to the last fashion of the Anglo-Saxon, there is a magnetic attraction that compels the stranger to linger and enjoy the kaleidoscopic scene. For three miles the change is continual, the continuity of effect is unbroken; and a walk up or down Broadway is one of the pleasantest reminiscences of a visit to the metropolis. Yonder is the famous and most comfortable St. Nicholas Hotel; a little farther up the immense brown-stone form of the Metropolitan Hotel, another of our fashionable hostelries. At the corner of Bond Street and Broadway is the artistic structure erected by Brooks Brothers, the clothiers, and nearly opposite is the Grand Central Hotel, a monster edifice, with a marble front eight stories in height and surmounted by a Mansard roof. Just around the corner, in Bond Street, is the spacious establishment of D. Appleton & Co., the publishers. It is, indeed, impossible to walk many yards without noticing one of the palaces with which the merchants have beautified the city. These, with the bustling cosmopolitan throng, make the thoroughfare one of such interest as not to be surpassed by anything in London or Paris.

The Approach to the East River Bridge.

It is a curious feature of the Broadway crowd, by-the-way, that its phases are different at different hours of the day. Early in the morning, for instance, you will see the working-people, the sewing-girls, and younger clerks, pouring into the street from right and left, and hurrying downward. At eight or nine o'clock the procession is chiefly composed of business-men—those who fill the counting-rooms and the law-offices. From ten to three the ladies appear in full force on shopping expeditions, and then the tide begins to turn upward. At four o'clock a hundred thousand are promenading; a goodly proportion being peripatetic fashion-plates, contrived by the cunning of the dress-maker and milliner. At six the poorer classes are again homeward bound; and then, until morning, Broadway is abandoned to the pleasure-seeker, midnight prowler, and poor wretches who have shunned the light of day.

The buildings occupied by the dry-goods and other firms on this part of Broadway are, as a rule, built of iron, modeled and painted to imitate white marble, though in a few cases the iron is designed to show for what it honestly is in its painting and gilding. Above Bleecker Street, on this great thoroughfare, the retail dealers in silks, satins, gloves, hosiery, articles of use, and ornaments of all descriptions, begin to multiply. Principal among the celebrated shops of New York is the retail dry-goods house of A. T. Stewart & Co., probably the largest establishment of the kind in the world, occupying a spacious marble building bounded by Ninth and Tenth Streets and Fourth Avenue. It instantly indicates itself to the stranger by the line of private carriages ranged in its front, and the cohort of coachmen and footmen waiting the advent of their mistresses. It is only by entering "Stewart's" that one can obtain an adequate idea of the immensity of the institution. If the eight floors of this building could be spread out on a level, they would occupy a space of fifteen acres. In this little world of trade there is nothing pertaining to the needs of a lady, from hairpins to the carpets with which she furnishes her boudoir, which may not be found in its proper department.

Among the minor parks of New York, Union Square is one of the most pretty and noted. Its extent is about three and a half acres, and it lies between Broadway and Fourth Avenue, and Fourteenth and Seventeenth Streets. It has a pleasant fountain in its center and a number of fine shade-trees, and during the summer season its benches are thronged with loungers, who while away the hours of the day in the shadow of the trees watching the mimic rainbow of the fountain. In the early morning and late afternoon, this, like all the other parks, is the resort of children and nurse-maids wheeling baby-carriages, and juvenile life lends to its aspect one of its prettiest features.

Statues of Washington and Lincoln face the park on the southeast and southwest corners respectively, and another, of Lafayette, is almost hidden in the foliage, opposite Broadway. On Decoration-day, May 30th, these monumental bronzes are richly wreathed with flowers. The equestrian statue of Washington was modeled by Browne, and is fourteen and a half feet in height, the entire monument, including the pedestal, being twenty-nine feet. This work has been generally and justly admired. The bronze statue of Abraham Lincoln, also by Browne, stands on a granite pedestal at the opposite angle of the square, and is an admirable likeness of the great original in form and feature. Perhaps the stiff citizen's garb in which the martyr-President is represented, though objectionable on account of rigidity of outline, better represents the awkward but stalwart personality than would a more artistic costume. The statue of Lafayette, also of bronze, was molded by the celebrated French sculptor Bartholdi, the projector of the Liberty statue to be erected on Bedloe's Island, and was the gift of the French Republic.

A paved plaza borders the park on the north along Seventeenth Street, where, on special occasions, a row of ornamental colored gas lamps are lighted. A cottage within the park facing the plaza has a balcony for the accommodation of reviewing officers of military parades, and it is also used as a platform for public speakers on the occasion of large mass-meetings. The park is a pleasant little oasis of greenery in the midst of a busy part of the city, and the rustling of the leaves, the twittering of the English sparrows—which are not only the faithful guardians of the trees in protecting them from the worms, but a never-ending source of amusement—and the tinkling of the fountain-spray as it falls back into the basin, make a soothing impression on the senses.

Twenty years ago, Union Square was a fashionable neighborhood, wherein resided many of the oldest and wealthiest families of New York; but it has yielded to the march of trade, and great changes have been made in its aspect. The fine old brown-stone mansions have been mostly torn down to make way for splendid business structures, and long before another decade has passed it will show an imposing array of architectural fronts. The surroundings of Union Square Park are of much

Broadway, south from the Post-Office.

interest, and in many ways make the locality attractive to the visitor. North of it is the Everett House, a famous old hostelry, which has entertained a large number of the most distinguished people who have passed through the city for the last quarter of a century. Opposite the Everett is the Clarendon Hotel, and several squares below, athwart the eastern side of the park, the Union Square Hotel, both favorite houses of entertainment. Near the corner of Broadway and Fourteenth Street is the Union Square Theatre, which, within the last seven years, has risen to share with Wallack's Theatre the honor of presenting to the public the most fashionable and artistic performances in the country, being devoted principally to the reproduction of Parisian successes, while Wallack's Theatre is most widely known as a theatre of comedy. The latter theatre, which for many years has had its home on the corner of Broadway and Thirteenth Street, will be moved the forthcoming season (1881) to the corner of Broadway and Thirty-first Street.

One square eastward of Union Square is the Academy of Music, in which have appeared the most celebrated contemporary singers. On a gala-night of the opera the adjacent streets even to the park itself are packed with carriages waiting the close of the performance. Union Square in the winter, on account of its importance as an amusement center, presents its most animated aspect from seven to eleven in the evening, after which it is nearly deserted, except by policemen and the late night-roisterers, who consider their day as just begun. That part of Fourteenth Street and Fourth Avenue directly opposite the statue of Washington is known in theatrical slang as the "slave-market," from the large number of actors always to be found lounging there in the summer, on the alert for an engagement.

On the west side of Union Square, corner of Fifteenth Street, is the splendid iron edifice of Tiffany & Co., the well-known jewelers and silversmiths, whose establishment is a grand museum of the most exquisite articles in jewels, gold and silver work, bronzes, statuary, bric-à-brac, and all the costly forms of ornament with which wealth delights to surround itself. Splendid equipages may be observed in front of this palace of art, which employs the finest skill of the Old and New World to delight its patrons from morning till night, and a continuous stream of richly-dressed women pours in and out. Nowhere in New York can the stranger pass an hour more agreeably than in viewing the art-treasures of this famous place, and nowhere is he likely to see the fashionable side of New York life more fully represented, except, perhaps, in the Academy of Music on a gala-night. Such are the principal attractions of Union Square Park and its environment, though it is probable that, within a few years, owing to inevitable changes, some of the surroundings which now give the locality so much of its charm will have ceased to exist.

Proceeding up the line of Broadway, which somewhat deflects at Fourteenth Street, the sight-seer passes by many fine buildings, and mingles in a varied stream of pedestrian life full of interest and movement. Brilliant shops devoted to jewelry, bric-à-brac, and ornamental goods, ladies' apparel, and fancy articles of every description, attract the eye, and the groups of well-dressed and handsome women standing at every show-window make the street-scene even more fascinating than the glowing colors shining behind the plate-glass. At Twenty-third Street, where Broadway and Fifth Avenue intersect, we reach Madison Square Park, the most delightful of the pleasances which exist in the heart of the city. This park includes about six acres, bounded by Broadway, Madison Avenue, Twenty-third and Twenty-sixth Streets, and it may be said to be the very heart of the world of amusement, gayety, and fashion.

The park abounds with fine shade-trees, has a large fountain, and its trim lawns are interspersed with splendid beds of flowers and vari-colored plants shaped in geometric designs. The numerous settees that border the walks are filled with a better class than one observes in the other minor city parks, the atmosphere of wealth and splendor which walls it in seeming unfavorable to the gathering together of the tramps and shiftless idlers who may be seen airing their tattered garments so often in the other parks. Many of the residents of the vicinity and the guests of the hotels may be observed reading their papers here of a bright spring or summer morning, and the air is musical with the prattle of rosy and beautiful children, accompanied by their white-capped bonnes. The trees are varied in character, large, and well-grown, and the care with which this park is kept makes it an exquisite and most refreshing bit of greenery and color. On the south side of the park, adjacent to the Broadway corner, a bronze statue of William H. Seward is seated on its pedestal, and on the upper western border the arm and torch-bearing hand of bronze, which will bear the lofty signal-flame of the Goddess of Liberty to be erected on

Union Square.

Madison Square and Twenty-third Street.

Bedloe's Island, is mounted for temporary display. The bronze statue of Admiral Farragut, which was erected in May, 1881, at the northwest corner of the park, is the work of the sculptor St. Gaudens, and represents the naval hero in uniform standing on a pyramidal pedestal. The attitude is one of stern sobriety and repose, and, in spite of the awkward lines of the straight-cut garments, the artist has succeeded in giving the figure a feeling of strength and dignity very noticeable. The decoration of the pedestal is elaborate and peculiar, giving various suggestions of the sea and its characteristic life, with much originality of treatment. On the Madison Square side of the park, again, a large and beautiful drinking-fountain has been recently placed, and the various stages and carriages which stop there for the horses to drink give a quaint and novel aspect to the scene.

The surroundings of the park are of the most striking character. In its immediate vicinity are eight or ten of the finest of the New York hotels, half a dozen clubs, the best restaurants, and several fine theatres, not to speak of the palatial residences on every hand. The march of trade has indeed invaded this region in great measure, aside from Broadway, which has always retained its commercial stamp; but the shops are so gay and elegant that they rather add to

than lessen the attractiveness of the *ensemble*. At the junction of Broadway and Fifth Avenue, opposite the park, stands a fine monument to the memory of Major-General Worth, a gallant soldier of the War of 1812, and the Seminole and Mexican campaigns.

Aside from the splendid houses of entertainment, such as the Fifth Avenue, Hoffman, Albemarle, Gilsey, Brunswick, etc., which are clustered in its near vicinity, and offer the stranger an *embarras de richesses* for his choice, we have Delmonico's Restaurant on the corner of Fifth Avenue and Twenty-sixth Street, and the Brunswick Restaurant at the northeast corner of the same streets. Both these famous places contribute largely to the life and activity of Madison Square, as they are frequented by the wealth, beauty, and fashion of New York to an extent not shared by any of their rivals. Delmonico's name has been a household word in the gastronomic world for many a long year, but during the last decade the Brunswick Restaurant has begun to compete with its widespread celebrity. The throngs of richly-dressed women and men that pour in and out of the doors of these palaces of the *cuisine* from early afternoon till late evening speak well for the culture of the gastronomic taste in America. The decorations of the Brunswick Restaurant are so unique and artistic as to be alone worth a visit. Dining here becomes an aesthetic as well as a physical pleasure, as the eye delights itself in the gold, black, and brown ornamentations of wall and ceiling, the pure crystal candelabra, the perennial foliage, the constant fountain, and the stained-glass windows.

The promenade in Madison Square on fine afternoons is full of animation, and all types of feminine beauty are aggregated in a fluttering stream of feathers and petticoats. Though all the women we see are not pretty, an entrancing proportion are, and a still larger proportion are attired with a discriminating liberality of taste which employs vivid color without a suggestion of gaudiness. Another characteristic is the vivacity of manner, and the abundant use of flowers, both natural and artificial, as a decoration. In the time of violets and roses, the air of this overheated city street is as fragrant as a garden. Nearly every woman wears a bouquet in her breast, and a perfect legion of sidewalk peddlers add to the sweetness with small bunches held out for sale in baskets and on trays.

At no time during the year are Fifth Avenue, Madison Square, Madison Avenue, and the other streets which concentrate in this beautiful portion of New York more attractive than in the month of May. The wealthy and fashionable classes do not begin to leave the city before the middle of June, so that in the month of blossoms we see the beauty and gayety of the *haut ton* disporting themselves under the pleasantest conditions.

Splendid equipages; handsomely-dressed women, buoyant with the atmosphere of genial May; fine-looking men, worthy successors of those whom Thackeray a quarter of a century since pronounced the most noble and distinguished-looking men in the world; throngs of beautiful children under the care of their nurses—present a bright and charming picture to the eye. Fifth-Avenuedom is then at its best, for the summer birds have not taken their flight, and find an irresistible temptation to live out-of-doors as much as possible. These gala-days of New York beauty and fashion last about a month, when the growing heat drives out of the city all who are not fastened by necessity. Mr. Wordsworth Thompson's painting of this scene, which we have engraved, was painted before the Farragut statue was erected, which stands in the Park nearly opposite the center of the picture.

Not far from Madison Square and the beginning of that great region where lives the "upper-tendom" of New York, is the art headquarters not only of the city, but the country. This association is a logical one, for more and more art tends to identify itself with fashion and fashionable ways. The days when the artist was a gay and rollicking Bohemian, disobedient to the conventions of society, have now pretty much disappeared; and the painter and sculptor study the purely commercial and social sides of their profession as shrewdly as does the shopkeeper, providing for the tastes, wise or otherwise, of the wealthy

Broadway, West Side of Madison Square.

classes who buy pictures, with the cautious pre-vision of the dealer in carpets or dress-patterns. The National Academy of Design is the fore-most art institution of the country, situated at the northwest corner of Fourth Avenue and Twenty-third Street, and an exhibition of new paintings is held in the spring of each year. The building, in an architectural sense, is one of the most striking in the city, full of notable archi-tectural features. The plan of the exterior was copied from a famous palace in Venice, and the gray and white marble and blue-stone used in its construction are beautifully blended. The front, on Twenty-third Street, is eighty feet long and extends on Fourth Avenue to a depth of ninety-eight feet nine inches. The double flight of steps leading to the main entrance has been skillfully made a part of the general design, and, with its beautiful carvings and drinking-fountain beneath, is unique. Within, the vestibule has a floor of variegated marbles leading up to the grand stair-way, which is massive and imposing. The third story is devoted entirely to the exhibition gal-leries, which are lighted from the roof. On the first and second stories are the offices, lecture-rooms, reception-room, and art schools. These schools are free, and are open from the first Monday in October in each year until the first of June the following year, continuously. All students first enter the antique school. Appli-cants for admission must file an application stat-ing name, address, place of nativity, what previ-ous training, if any, a reference as to personal character, etc., upon a blank form obtained on application to the Corresponding Secretary of the Academy. The applicant must submit to the Council a shaded drawing from a cast of some part of the human figure, which, if approved, will secure admission to the antique class, from which pupils are advanced to the life class upon executing in the school an approved drawing of a full-length statue. Oil- and water-colors may be used by permission of the professor in charge. Punctual attendance is required, under a penalty of forfeiture of membership; but members may attend one or all of the morning, afternoon, and night sessions, as they elect upon entering. The schools are open to both sexes, and the principles of art are taught through the study of antique sculpture and the living model, both nude and draped, by means of lectures on anatomy, per-spective, and other subjects, through portrait, sketch, and composition classes, and in such other ways as are from time to time provided. The first three days of the spring exhibitions are known as artists'-day, varnishing-day, and pri-

vate-view. Admission on the last of these days is eagerly sought, and cards of invitation are sent to the leading people of New York society. At such times the Academy of Design is thronged with the beauty and wealth of New York soci-ety, and the richly-attired gathering makes al-most as brilliant a show as the pictures on the walls, which nominally the people come to see. A younger institution, the Society of American Artists, is progressing with such lusty vigor that, though as yet it has no permanent home, it prom-ises by-and-by to equal if not surpass the parent trunk of which it is an offshoot.

Directly opposite the Academy of Design, at the southwest corner of Fourth Avenue and Twenty-third Street, is the building of the Young Men's Christian Association, a highly-ornamental structure to this part of the city. It is among the finest specimens of the Renaissance style of architecture in the metropolis. The roof is of the steep Mansard pattern, presenting towers of equal height at each corner of the building, and a large tower (windowed) over the entrance on Twenty-third Street. The material is New Jer-sey brown-stone and the yellowish marble from Ohio, in almost equal parts, the latter composing the decorative portion. The building contains twenty-five apartments, including gymnasium, library, lecture-rooms, offices, etc.

Let us now retrace our steps and scan the be-ginnings of a street which has a reputation as wide as the civilized world, and has given name to a great social force in American life—Fifth Avenue. Leaving Broadway and proceeding through Waverley Place, three short squares bring us to Washington Square. The park, which is a beautiful one, shaded with very large, full trees, has two fountains, and is a highly picturesque and attractive resort, from its surroundings, though the current of fashion has long since passed north-ward. On the east side the New York University Building lifts its castellated bastions and turrets like some old mediæval donjon, and lends a pecul-iar aspect of old-fashioned quaintness to the scene. During the genial summer days this spot of shade and verdure is much patronized by those waifs and strays of humanity who are either too lazy to work or are unable to obtain it, and the knights of rags and tatters may be observed here smok-ing their pipes philosophically during the day-time, or reposing on the benches at night, in larger numbers than anywhere else in the city. The curious observer of human nature can find in the flotsam and jetsam of human wreck, who float in here as in some quiet cove, a wonderful field for pursuing his favorite study, as all grades

"A May-Day in Fifth Avenue" (From a Painting by Wordsworth Thompson.)

of poverty and shiftlessness are well represented. The park is also a favorite play-ground for children, and their bright faces and active little figures lend a cheery look to what might otherwise be the too grim forlornness of the tramp and idler. The north side of Washington Square is peculiarly impressive and interesting, from the style of the residences, many of which are still inhabited by rich old families too much in love with past associations, and the beauty of the location, to yield to the behests of fashion. The houses are built of red brick with white-marble trimmings and marble stoops. The peculiarly bright and refreshing aspect of such houses in the wilderness of brown-stone can hardly be described too enthusiastically; and, as they are for the most part kept with the most perfect clean-liness and taste, the pedestrian lingers here with a sense of warm appreciation of what may be called an old-fashioned novelty.

Fifth Avenue, perhaps the most famous street in America as the representative locality in which for more than thirty years fashionable New York has expended its love of lavish display, begins at the center of Washington Square. The wealth and social pride of New York have had their strongholds at Bowling Green, East Broadway, Bond and Bleecker Streets, and Washington Square, respectively. Now Fifth Avenue is the successor, and where the next grand concentration of the aristocracy of money will be it is not easy to forecast.

Fifth Avenue is a broad, straight avenue running to Fifty-ninth Street, thence along the east

Twenty-third Street from corner of Fourth Avenue.
(Young Men's Christian Association Building on the left; National Academy of Design on the right.)

side of Central Park, and to Mount Morris at One Hundred and Twentieth Street, which breaks its continuity. It begins again at One Hundred and Twenty-fourth Street, and runs to the Harlem River. Probably there is not another street in the world wherein are more elegant and imposing private residences, furnished with princely magnificence, or more exquisite collections of those trifles of art and taste which bespeak a high order of cultivation. From the southern terminus to Central Park, a distance of two and a half miles, it presents an unbroken array of splendid dwellings and noble churches, with exception of here and there in its lower portion where business establishments which deal for example in musical instruments, pictures, jewelry, and articles of a costly and or-namental character, have encroached on its fashionable private character. Many of the edifices in this long stretch of palatial domiciles possess marked beauty of architectural design, and all of them are built in massive and splendid blocks for the most part of brown-stone. In spite of the uniformity of appearance, which comes of a general use of the same building material and a similar style of structure, sufficient variety and character are given the street by the numerous splendid church edifices and the few hotels and private dwellings of a differing style of architecture to relieve the somber and massive dignity which would otherwise stamp the aspect of the street.

It would be impracticable to describe in detail the many objects of interest which are to

Fifth Avenue Scenes.

Fifth Avenue, at corner of Twenty-first Street.

be seen on this avenue: to penetrate its huge club-houses, its large and expensive libraries, choice picture-galleries, private billiard-rooms, and exquisitely furnished parlors, and a drive over its Belgian pavement, and a glance at the exterior features of the street, must suffice.

The real glory of the avenue is to be seen best on Sunday after the morning service. Fashion in all its strangest conglomerations and beauty in its most striking attire then exhibit themselves on the promenade. The street is also a favorite highway for the owners of equipages en route to and from the Park, and every pleasant afternoon witnesses a display of showy animals and vehicles almost unequaled, certainly not surpassed, in Europe or America. Next to a fashionable race-course it is the place above all others in New York for the exhibition of handsome horse-flesh.

Nearly every square in Fifth Avenue presents something of interest to the eye of the stranger. At the corner of Eighth Street is the Brevoort House, an aristocratic family hotel, which is more largely patronized by wealthy foreigners than any other hostelry in the city. At the corner of Fifteenth Street is the Manhattan Club, famous as the political headquarters of what is known in the expressive slang of the day as the

"swallow-tail democracy," and immediately opposite are to be noticed the massive walls of the Haight apartment-house, for a long time, before the French-flat system had got such a stronghold in New York, the most splendid establishment of the kind in the city.

At the corner of Twenty-first Street are the Union and Lotos Clubs, the former embracing a greater aggregate of wealth among its members than any club in the city, and the latter the well-known resort of the art and literary professions. At the corner of Eighteenth Street are the splendid Music Hall and Warerooms of Chickering & Co., the piano-forte manufacturers, and a few blocks below are the piano-showrooms of Weber and Knabe. Knoedler's art-store and picture-gallery, a branch of Goupil's of Paris, attracts the eye on the corner of Twenty-second Street. Here the visitor to New York always finds a delightful place for whiling away half an hour, and it is a convenient stopping-place on the way up Fifth Avenue.

Passing through Madison Square, which has been described previously, we continue our way up the magnificent avenue, finding continual food to attract the eye and excite the interest. The window-fronts we shall find during the summer months decorated with tiled flower-boxes, laden with a perfect glory of blooms in all the colors of the rainbow. This is a charming characteristic of the leading residence streets in the aristocratic portion of the city, and speaks volumes for the taste and love of beauty inherent even among those who may have made their money so suddenly as to be without the social and æsthetic culture which makes wealth the most enjoyable. Fifth Avenue is exceptionally noticeable for this lavish display of flowers on the window-ledges, that seem to be literally blossoming out of the brown-stone a little distance away.

When we reach the corner of Thirty-fourth Street, the eye is instantly arrested by the stately marble palace built by the late A. T. Stewart, until recently justly regarded as the most costly and luxurious private residence on the continent. The reception and drawing rooms, the dining, breakfast, and sleeping rooms, are very beautiful in decoration and furnishing. We are now in a region of an almost unbroken line of architectural beauty; handsome churches and mansions abound, and the wonderful changes that are taking place in the upper portion of New York are written on every side. Superb mansions are continually being pulled down to make way for structures still more palatial, and the rage for surpassing each other in the splendor of their domiciles seems to have taken possession of our merchant, banker, and railroad princes.

The magnificent mansions built by members of the Vanderbilt family, of which we give an engraving on the next page, on the square between Fifty-first and Fifty-second Streets, on Fifth Avenue, and on the northwestern corner of Fifty-second Street, may be regarded as the finest houses in New York. Those occupying the first-named square are of brown-stone, elaborately carved and ornamented. They are connected together by a gallery into which the main entrance leads. The house on the upper Fifty-second Street corner is built of light-gray stone, and is most artistic and unique in its architectural front. Another member of the Vanderbilt family is building a grand house of red brick, with heavy trimmings of gray stone, at the upper corner of Fifth Avenue and Fifty-seventh Street. These noble structures rank among the finest private residences in the world.

At no time is there more animation in Fifth Avenue than on the day when the Coaching Club makes its annual parade, which occurs on the last Saturday in May. Every door and window on the most brilliant of our streets is pictorial with the faces of handsome women, and crowds of the *jeunesse dorée* of both sexes assemble at every place of vantage to wait the enlivening show of the four-in-hands as they dash by. The Coaching Club was instituted in

Thirty-fourth Street, corner of Fifth Avenue.

New York in 1876, for the purpose of encouraging four-in-hand driving. There are now twenty-six members, representing twenty-one coaches. The meet is always in front of the the most enlivening kind as the coaches dash off at speed, the guards sounding the "Tally-ho!" on their long horns. This brisk music is kept up from time to time during the trip, and the long-drawn, mellow notes appear to add fresh fire to the horses as well as animation to the gay chatter of the charming and stylishly-dressed beauties who sit on the boxes and fill the top seats in company with the gentlemen drivers. To be invited to ride on such an occasion is a brevet of fashionable eminence, dear to the heart of every woman who sighs to shine in the glittering van of social life.

Fifth Avenue.—The Vanderbilt Mansion.

Four-in-hand coaching has thriven marvelously since its first institution in New York, but it is not a thing indigenous to the soil, and probably will never quite arouse the genuine enthusiasm which it evokes in the land where it is "native to the manner born." It has its root in the instincts of that large class of wealthy young men who have bravely set themselves to remodeling the crudities of American society by the British standard, and believe that "nothing good can come out of Nazareth." It is even said by certain satirists that some of these Anglo-maniacs cultivate the misplacement of the h's, but this is probably a libel. However the coaching fever may have been an exotic, it certainly develops some picturesque features of life which are not without their pleasant side.

Hotel Brunswick, corner of Fifth Avenue and Twenty-seventh Street, and the route through Fifth Avenue and the Park, thence down the avenue again to Washington Square, and back again to the starting-place. The scene is of While the Club as such only parades once a year, individual members show their drags, and strive to witch the feminine world by the way they handle their ribbons, nearly every fine day in the Park during the spring and early summer. Some

Coaching Day.—Scene in Fifth Avenue.

of them are always to be seen at the Jerome
Park races, and during the summer months at
Newport—that most fashionable and exclusive
of watering-places.

The origin of the Coaching Club appears to
have been in the enterprise of Colonel Delan-
cey Kane, who startled the New York world
in 1875 by running a coach daily between the
Brunswick Hotel and Castle Inn, New Rochelle,
in imitation of the young English aristocrats, who
had taken in similar manner to becoming public
Jehus.   This noble example quickly inspired
other rich owners and lovers of horse-flesh, and
several regular excursions were announced, but

only to be withdrawn afterward, the original
instigator of this character of enterprise having
been the only one to carry it out systematically,
though a regular club of coaching experts was
formed.   It is understood that a large number
of the gilded youths who belong to the London
coaching clubs do act as drivers on several delightful excursion routes out of London, and are
thus the means of bestowing genuine pleasure on
that portion of the public who love the breezy
downs, the stately hedgerows, and the swiftly
changing forms of summer pomp and beauty to
be enjoyed behind four splendid roadsters; but
so far the enthusiasm of the Coaching Club of

Fifth Avenue and Fifty-sixth Street.

New York seems in only one case to have settled
into this useful form.

As we approach Central Park on Fifth Avenue the stately and palatial homes of our rich
men do not show in the least any declension
from the dignity of the street—many of them,
indeed, displaying unique and striking characteristics not observable farther down town.   The
beautiful architecture of the porches, which
will be more specially referred to in another
place, catches the eye instantly, and indicates
the operation of a certain individuality of taste,
which does not rest content with mere splendid commonplace, but struggles to express that

conception of a home which makes both the
exterior and interior of the temple wherein is
set the shrine of one's household gods the outcome of adjustment between the dwelling and
the dwellers.

The fine residence square at Fifth Avenue and
Fifty-sixth Street, built of Caen-stone, though
not specially noticeable in its architectural ornament, attracts attention from the happy union
of lightness with the idea of mass and dignity.
The low, roomy porches, the broad windows,
and the Mansard roofs, give a genial, home-like
aspect to these edifices, which more lavish expenditure might sometimes fail to attain.   In

Park Avenue.

this portion of the street adjoining the park one can not help observing the charming appearance of the sidewalks on a bright, sunshiny day, created by the great number of children going to and from the park, from boys and girls rolling their hoops and spinning their tops, to baby-carriages laden with their infant freight and wheeled by nurses.

The street immediately east of Fifth Avenue, Madison Avenue, rivals the former for about two miles in the number and elegance of its fashionable residences. Beginning at Madison Square, its homes, its churches, and its clubhouses are of the same splendid character already noticed, until we approach Central Park. Here it still retains something of the roughness of a new thoroughfare. Probably in the course of another year this noble avenue will be complete, when it will be unsurpassed for the imposing character of its architecture.

Strolling eastward from Madison Avenue, we next come to a street of exceptional charm and attractiveness in Park Avenue, as that portion of Fourth Avenue which lies between Thirty-

Elevated Railway on Third Avenue.

fourth Street and the Grand Central Railway Station is called. It is almost in the center of Murray Hill, the ultra-fashionable portion of the city, and yet its position isolates it from the bustle and the noise to which both Fifth and Madison Avenues are subjected. This thoroughfare is built over the tunnel of the Fourth Avenue Railway line, and this peculiarity of position, united with the great width of the street, makes possible the highly ornamental and effective character of its *ensemble*.

At regular intervals in the center of the avenue are neatly railed inclosures of green sod, with grated apertures through which light and air are supplied to the tunnel beneath. These miniature parks (whence the name of the avenue) are planted with shrubs which have already attained a fine growth, and in some cases flowers; and they give the aspect of the thoroughfare an indescribably peaceful and rustic charm, which exists in no other New York street located in the heart of the city. Fine roadways run on

Corner of Sixth Avenue and Twenty-third Street, showing Elevated Railway and Station.

either side of the center, and here we observe a noble display of carriages on a pleasant day. Park Avenue has for some time been a favorite location with our wealthy people, and only its shortness prevents it from being a street which would more than rival the other aristocratic localities of the city in its repute as a representative home of wealth and social prestige.

Near the northwest corner of Thirty-fourth Street and Park Avenue is the Presbyterian Church of the Covenant, built in the Lombardo-Gothic style, and at the corner of Thirty-third Street is the Park Avenue Hotel, which is one of the finest of New York hostelries. Without attempting to enumerate in detail the numerous fine structures on this avenue, we must content ourselves with calling attention to the generally unique aspect of its appearance, which challenges admiration as something apart from all other thoroughfares in the Empire City.

Nothing contributes more to give characteristic quality to the street-scenes of New York, on several of its streets and avenues, than the elevated railway system, which is found in no other city of the world. Whether it has improved the appearance of the portions of the city through which it passes is a matter of individual opinion; but assuredly the change is a most notable one. At the outset there was bitter opposition on the part of shopkeepers and householders, but this has for the most part subsided; and it is now generally acknowledged that business in Third and Sixth Avenues, which are the most intimately affected by the elevated roads, has been improved by what first threatened to be a detriment.

Apart from all other considerations, it is generally conceded that the vexed problem of rapid transit has been solved in a practical and efficient manner. The long and narrow conformation of the city renders comparatively few lines necessary, and obviates for the most part the dangers and difficulties which might arise from frequent junctions and street-crossings. The first line in this rapid-transit system to be constructed was the old Greenwich Street and Ninth Avenue road, on the west side, the motive-power of which was originally designed to be by stationary engines, but these soon gave way to locomotives. This line was vastly improved by the construction of a double track from South Ferry, at the extreme southern end of the city, to Central Park. The same corporation has also built a double-track road on the east side, from the City Hall (just opposite which is to be the entrance of the stone causeway of the East River Bridge) to Chatham Square, and thence through the Bowery and Third Avenue, along which thoroughfare it extends to Harlem and One Hundred and Twenty-ninth Street. The structure varies according to the character of the street in which it is located. Front and Pearl being narrow, the roadway is bridged from curb to curb by transverse lattice-girders; the Bowery being wide, the tracks are carried upon separate rows of pillars on each side of the street; while on Third Avenue they are erected upon a line of columns at each side of the street-car tracks, and connected at the top by light, open, elliptic arch-girders. A clear idea of the different structures and the rolling-stock may be obtained from our illustrations.

To the business-man, living far up town, the elevated roads are so valuable that he now wonders how he could have dispensed with them so long. As a mode of access to theatres and other places of amusement their importance grows with immense strides. The value of real estate has been largely enhanced in the up-town districts, and building greatly stimulated. The effects of these roads have only begun to be fully appreciated by the public.

The Metropolitan Elevated Railway, on the west side, begins at the rear of Trinity Church and runs to Central Park—the route being through New Church Street, Church Street, Murray Street, College Place, West Broadway, South Fifth Avenue, Amity Street, and Sixth Avenue, to the park. At Fifty-third Street a branch debouches to Ninth Avenue, whence it proceeds to One Hundred and Tenth Street, crosses to Eighth Avenue, and thence extends to the Harlem River (One Hundred and Fifty-fifth Street). Until recently this was the terminus of the road, but the completion of the bridge across the Harlem River now enables the trains to connect with the New York City & Northern Railroad, for High Bridge, Fordham, Yonkers, Tarrytown and other points, to Brewsters, five miles distant. The equipment of this road is excellent. The cars are duplicates of the Pullman palace-cars. The seats have spring cushions, upholstered with brown morocco leather, and are placed two-by-two at each side of the aisle, except at the ends, where they are ranged longitudinally around the car, the object of this arrangement being to leave enough space near the doors for the ingress and egress of passengers. The windows are wide and high, and are of plate-glass with adjustable up-blinds. The exteriors are a very delicate shade of green. The stations, designed by the celebrated landscape artist, J. F. Cropsey, are all that could be desired. The average length of the platforms is one hundred and thirty feet, the average width

The West Side Elevated Railroad at 110th Street.

West Street, near Canal Street.

eleven feet, and the average height twenty feet. The passengers reach them by three short flights of steps, covered by pavilion roofs, and lighted by suspended gas-lamps. At the head of the steps there is a balcony, from which the passengers enter a ticket-office leading to the platform, and at each side of the entrance there is a waiting-room—one for ladies and the other for gentlemen. The waiting-rooms are furnished with black walnut, and finished with yellow pine touched and stained with variegated colors; lighted by gas, heated and provided with separate toilet and retiring rooms. The platform is covered from end to end by a pavilion roof, the lines of which are picturesquely broken by wrought-iron crestings and finials, which give the whole structure a graceful and uncommon appearance.

The Second Avenue Elevated line, which is a branch of the Metropolitan Elevated Railway Company, extends from the Battery to Harlem River, and it is ultimately proposed that it shall cross the river on a bridge to be built, and have its terminus, at some point not yet fixed, in Westchester County. The cars used on the branches of the Metropolitan Elevated Railway are far more comfortable and elegant than those used on the Ninth and Third Avenue lines, which constitute the New York Elevated. Both the roads, including the four lines, have within the last two years been leased to a corporation

known as the Manhattan Company, the object having been to harmonize conflicting interests and secure uniformity of management.

The most striking impression made on the mind by the Elevated Railroads, as an example of skillful and audacious engineering, is at One Hundred and Tenth Street, between Eighth and Ninth Avenues. Here the substructure attains the remarkable height of sixty-three feet, and the massive iron beams and girders, owing to their great elevation, appear too frail to bear the burden imposed on them. As one drives under this giant curved bridge, and sees the trains gliding far over his head in the air, the imagination is fascinated with the thought of the daring of science which overcomes the greatest difficulties by the precision and thoroughness with which it adapts its means to its ends.

The fare on all the roads from the lower termini to the Harlem River is ten cents, except between the hours of 4.30 and 7.30 in the evening, and the same hours relatively in the morning. From South Ferry to Central Park the running time is about twenty-five minutes. "What is there to prevent the train from tumbling into the street?" asks a timid reader. Within each rail, and higher than it, is an exceedingly strong timber firmly bolted to the cross-ties, and the plan of the tracks is such that, in case of any breakage of wheel or axle, the body of the cars can only fall a few inches before it comes in contact with this guard, which also holds the wheels against the track. A better criterion than this of the safety of the system is the fact that there have been so few accidents, and nearly all of these in the case of employees, become bold and reckless through long custom. Without any clamor, straining, or ringing of bells, the train glides out of the station along the track, running between stations at the rate of about thirty miles an hour, and making, with stoppages, about twelve miles an hour. It is controlled by atmospheric breaks and electric signals, and can

South Street below Burling Slip.

Market-Wagons Stand.

be brought to a standstill in a little more than its own length. The stoppages are made with scarcely any jolting, and with very little delay. The platforms at the rear and front are inclosed by iron railings and gates, which are not opened until the train is still, and are closed the moment it moves again. Such is the Rapid-Transit System of New York, which probably could not be surpassed in its general adaptation to the needs of the city and people.

No student of New York street-life can afford to overlook some of the busy and character-istic scenes which are to be observed in those business localities adjacent to the wharves and docks, where the shipping interests create an activity and atmosphere peculiar to themselves. The streets, always the dirtiest and most un-sightly in New York, perhaps necessarily so, are choked up with heavy drays, trucks, baggage and freight wagons, so that the chaos seems al-most inextricable. The roughest of the laboring classes find employment in these regions, and sulphurous oaths may be heard at every turn, em-phasized from time to time by a furious fisticuff combat. The low "dives" and drinking-shops that infest these streets contribute largely to the confusion, and help to make an active supervision of the police more necessary than elsewhere. The importance of the business represented in the bustle and movement of such thoroughfares as West Street on the North River front, and South Street on the East River front, can hardly be over-estimated. Over the ferries which cross the North River pours a constant tide of passengers and freight. Nearly all the great railways have their freight-depots either in Jersey City or at the North River wharves of the New York side, and the immensity of traffic is eloquently suggested in the turmoil and tangle of the express and baggage wagons, and the drays and trucks constantly arriving and departing. When we cross to the East River front, we reach the locality where the world's commerce declares itself

Tenement-Houses.

in a forest of tall masts. Here again we have confusion worse confounded in the sights and sounds of street-life, but, beneath the apparent chaos and disorder, the machinery which moves the business world and puts forth its invisible connections to every part of the land works with the unfailing force of some ponderous engine.

While touching those sides of New York life which have a picturesqueness all their own, we must not omit to call attention to the appearance of the whole congeries of streets in the vicinity of the block bounded by West, Little Twelfth,

Washington, and Gansevoort Streets, known as the Market-Wagon Stand, in the early morning, when the market-wagoners fetch in their produce from the country. For nearly a mile within a block or two of the water-front the thoroughfares are packed close with the wagons from which New York draws its supply of vegetables. Farmers, gardeners, and huckster-women, with wholesome tan on the hands and faces, make the early hours busy with their traffic, and bring to the air of the city the scent of the green fields and flowers of the rural districts. By 7 A. M., however, these country visitors have all departed, and the city again resumes its furious life of toil and trade.

While the sight-seer amuses himself with studying the aspects of life and business adjoining the water-line of New York, he may, if he will, penetrate in a short walk to the heart of the tenement house region, where poverty and wretchedness present their most distressing forms. The vilest groggeries are sown thick on every block, and reeling men and women illustrate the threadbare moral as old as the world, that vice and misery go hand in hand. A glance at the region of rookeries, however, suffices, and we will pass to pleasanter scenes. With a brief reflection. Attempts have been made to solve the problem of model tenement-houses for the poor, but in a very imperfect way. Both in London and Paris systematic efforts have been made with fair success in this direction. New York philanthropy should follow this noble example.

BUILDINGS.

City Hall and New Court-House.

NEW YORK, as behooves the greatest and most populous city of the New World, and one of the richest capitals on the globe, abounds, at every hand, with noble buildings, public and private, the latter of which compare favorably with those of any of the centers of the Old-World civilization. It goes without saying that we can not boast of those time-worn and picturesque old edifices which are the delight of the artist, and appeal so powerfully to the historic imagination. But, aside from these heritages of former ages, which add so much to the fascination of European capitals, the metropolis of America is in many ways notable for the striking character of its architecture.

The City Hall, wherein is located the headquarters of the Municipal Government, stands in the Park, between the Post-Office and the County Court-House, and was erected between the years 1803 and 1812, at a cost of more than half a million dollars, the location then being on the outskirts of the city. The edifice is of white marble, with a rear wall of brown-stone,

in the Italian style, the dimensions being two hundred and sixteen feet long by one hundred and five deep. It contains the Mayor's office, Common Council Chamber, and other city offices, and the City Library. The "Governor's Room," on the second floor, is used for official receptions, and it contains the desk on which George Washington penned his first message to Congress, the chairs used by the first Congress, the chair in which Washington was inaugurated first President of the United States, and a gallery of paintings, embracing portraits of many of the mayors of the city, State Governors, and leading national officers and Revolutionary chieftains, mostly by well-known artists. The building is surmounted by a cupola containing a four-dial clock, which is illuminated at night by gas. This building has been the scene of many noteworthy episodes in city, State, and national affairs. Although the first of the important public buildings erected in New York, it is generally conceded to be unexcelled in purity and beauty of design.

The New Court-House, which stands close at

hand, will, when fully completed, be a structure fully worthy of a great municipal corporation. It is constructed of white marble, and, in all its details, interior and exterior, unites strength, elegance, and solidity. The prevailing order of architecture is Corinthian, and the general effect of its proportions is striking. The structure is three stories in height, two hundred and fifty feet long by one hundred and fifty feet wide, and the crown of the dome is to be two hundred and ten feet above the sidewalk. It has been suggested that the tower crowning the dome should be converted into a lighthouse as a landmark for mariners, but this point has not been, so far, fully decided. The portico and steps, with the grand columns, on the Chambers Street front, are said to be the finest piece of work of the kind in America. The interior of the edifice is equally elaborate and complete, the beams and staircases being of iron, and the finishing of hard wood. The State Courts and several of the city departments have their headquarters in the building. There was a good deal of scandal connected with the erection of the building, as it was one of the chief vehicles of peculation by the " Ring " in 1869-'70, large sums appropriated for its construction finding their way into the pockets of the existing city officials. The dome shown in the illustration has not yet been erected.

Among the notable public buildings, the Custom-House, on the corner of Wall and William Streets, attracts attention from its solid and massive appearance. This edifice, formerly the Merchants' Exchange, is a huge pile of Quincy granite, two hundred by one hundred and sixty feet, and seventy-seven feet high. The Wall Street portico has twelve front, four middle, and two rear columns, each of granite, thirty-eight feet high, and four and a half feet in diameter. The rotunda is eighty feet high, and the dome is supported on eight pilasters of fine Italian variegated marble. The cost of the building and ground was one million eight hundred thousand dollars. It is said to be entirely inadequate for its present use, so rapidly has the commerce of the port of New York expanded, and the erection of a new custom-house has been strongly urged.

The most imposing of the public edifices of New York is the Post-Office and United States Court Building, at the junction of Park Row and Broadway. No post-office building in the world, we believe, exceeds this in size. The only materials used in its construction are granite, iron, brick, and glass; the former coming from an island off the coast of Maine. The style of architecture adopted is that known as the Doric, modified, however, by the Renaissance. The north front of the building is two hundred and ninety feet in length, the Broadway front three hundred and forty feet, and the Park Row front

Custom-House, Wall Street.

Post Office, and U. S. Court Building.

three hundred and twenty feet in the clear. On each of these two fronts, however, there is an angle which, running back some distance, and then projecting, forms the entrance looking down Broadway. The entire width of this front is one hundred and thirty feet. These entering angles and projecting portico give this front a very bold and striking appearance. In the original design it was intended that the building should have a cellar, a basement, three stories, and also an attic; but, through an after-thought of the architect, a fourth story has been added. The roof is of the Mansard style, the upright portion being covered with slate, and the flat portion with copper. In accordance with the plans of the architect, the basement consists of one vast department, which is devoted to the sorting of letters and making up of the mails.

The first floor is used as the receiving department; comprising the money-order and registering offices, stamp and envelope bureaus, and postmaster's and secretaries' private rooms. On the second and third floors are the United States Court rooms, and the attic supplies rooms to the janitor, watchmen. etc. There are no fewer than twelve elevators for the various purposes of the establishment, and for light and heat the most perfect contrivances known to art have been adopted. It was completed in the summer of 1875, and first occupied September 1st of that year.

We derive from an article in "Scribner's Magazine" a few interesting statistics. About one hundred and thirty-four million letters, etc., are delivered annually, and an equal number are sent away. Over twelve hundred men are em-

Interior, Post-Office.

City Prison, or "The Tombs."

ployed, and communication is kept up with nearly thirty-six thousand offices.

As the letters are consigned to the mail through the various "drops" in the corridors, they are "faced up" or put with all their directed sides facing the same way. As fast as they fall upon a table a man prepares them for the stamper, and after the stamper comes the separator, who puts the letters for each mail together; after him the mail-maker takes a hand and verifies every letter in each mail, ties them into a bundle and puts on each a printed label marked with its destination, and stamped with his own name. When the packages are opened on the postal car, the route agent marks whatever errors there may be in them upon the labels and returns these to the New York Post-Office. A rigid account of these errors is kept, and every man's percentage of correctness for a given time is set opposite his name, on a sheet that is conspicuously posted in the office. Some men have become so accurate that they will have for several months a clean record, not having made a single mistake in the mailing of a letter. This accuracy is one of the tests upon which the salaries are graded from time to time, and there is, consequently, the liveliest emulation in the matter.

When the mail-maker has tied up his letters they go to the poucher, who assorts them, throw-ing the several packages with unerring aim into their several divisions, arranged like large pigeon-holes in a semicircular form. These pigeon-holes slope downward toward the back, and, even while the poucher is throwing, the dispatcher may be affixing the pouches at the back, opening a sliding door and emptying the mail into the bags, which are immediately locked and sent off to the wagons which take them to the railway-depots.

Of the whole number—nearly a hundred and fifty millions of letters and packages a year at this time—about one half are distributed through boxes at the central office, about one fourth by carriers, and about one fourth are sent to the stations in other parts of the city. Every letter received here is stamped at once with the hour of its arrival. All letters coming in between ten and eleven o'clock in the morning are stamped "11 A. M." When the hour turns, the stamper wipes his stamp clean of ink, lays it away in a drawer and takes a new one with the next hour upon it and proceeds again. The greatest care is exercised to have the stamp legible.

At the hour of departure of the carriers, the delivery department is full of animation; the men in their uniforms pass from one assorter's table to another and take, each from his own box, all the mail deposited therein, while the impassive assorter goes right on throwing mail into the box for the next delivery. Then you will see the carriers at a long counter, which is divided by little raised partitions into compartments, each making his mail into a conveniently-arranged bundle.

In the New York office the accounts of incoming and outgoing letters are carefully balanced like a cash balance every evening, and not a man is allowed to leave the department if the balance is not correct. One night the men were kept until nearly morning looking for a letter that had dropped through a crack in an old table, and lodged in the folds of a worn-out mail-bag, and so got kicked into a corner during the search. At another time, when the office was at its wit's end after a night of search, it was found that an absent-minded man had carefully deposited his pen in the safe, and put the missing package in the pen's place in his table-drawer.

The northern end of the Post-Office fronts upon the City Hall Park, which is identified with the early history and growth of New York. Less than a century ago it was looked upon as the "Old Fields," and the country residences of wealthy citizens were erected in and around the adjacent grounds. A portion of the walls of the present Hall of Records constituted, as far back as 1758, the walls of the colonial provost jail, and many an incident might be related of the dark and bloody scenes enacted on the spot. Within the last ten years the Park has undergone much change, and, with its shrubbery, trees, fountains, and broad walks, it now constitutes an attractive feature of this portion of the metropolis.

Were it not that the Tombs, as the City Prison of New York is commonly called, is so unfortunately located, it would be one of the most

Court-House, Sixth Avenue and Tenth Street.

U. S. Barge Office, Battery.

striking and impressive buildings of the metropolis. It is an admirable specimen of Egyptian architecture, and the gloomy majesty of its aspect assorts well with its character as a temple of woe and misery, for here have been performed for nearly half a century all the tragedies of justice which have taken place in the city. The building is a large one, occupying the entire square bounded by Centre Street on the east, Elm Street on the west, Leonard Street on the south, and Franklin Street on the north, but its really grand proportions are greatly dwarfed by its situation, which is in a deep hollow, so that the top of its massive walls scarcely rises above the level of Broadway, which is about one hundred yards distant from the western façade.

The site was formerly occupied by the "Collect Pond," a sheet of water connected with the Hudson or North River by a strip of swamp through which ran a little rivulet on a line with the present Canal Street, which derives its name from this circumstance. The pond was filled up in 1836, and the prison erected on it within two years. The soil, being marshy, was ill calculated to bear the weight of the solid structure, and, despite the fact that the foundations were laid deeper than was customary, some parts of the wall settled so much that fears were entertained for the safety of the entire building. It has now stood for over a third of a century, however,

without any noticeable change, and is considered perfectly safe. The name of "Tombs" it has had ever since its erection, and was given to it in consequence of its then damp and unhealthy condition, and of its generally gloomy appearance. Externally the building is entirely of granite, and appears as one lofty story, the windows being carried from a point about two yards above the ground up to beneath the cornice. The main entrance is on Centre Street, and is reached by a flight of wide, dark stone steps, through an exceedingly lugubrious but spacious portico supported by four massive columns. The external walls on the other three sides are more or less broken up by projecting entrances and columns or insertions, infusing at least some degree of variety into the heavy monotone of the style. The Court of Special Sessions and a police court are held in the building. Internally the prison is rather a series of buildings than a single structure. The cells rise in tiers one above the other, with a separate corridor for each row. Besides those awaiting trial in the Special Sessions and police courts, persons accused or convicted of the more heinous crimes are confined here until they have been tried before the higher courts, or until they depart for the State Prison, or are ready for the gallows, which is erected in the interior quadrangle of the prison, whenever an execution is to take place. The visitor experiences a sense of relief as he hears the last echo of his footsteps reverberating among the gloomy passages and resumes his walk in the sunshine.

One of the most ornamental of the buildings devoted to the uses of justice is the Court-House at the intersection of Sixth and Greenwich Avenues and West Tenth Street, which is the seat of the Third District Court. The edifice is both picturesque and cheerful in its aspect, and would not be associated with its true function by the casual observer, if it were not for the police-officers, who may be generally seen lounging on its steps or passing in and out of its doors. The architecture is of a composite nature, showing characteristics of the Byzantine and Renaissance, but tastefully harmonized. Among our minor public buildings, there is none more attractive than this, and it is to be hoped that the city will always be as fortunate in using its money to as much advantage in the erection of edifices, alike decorative and well fitted to its uses.

The new United States Barge-Office, which is an appurtenance of the Custom-House, is located on the Battery, adjoining the Staten Island Ferry-House. It is a solid and well-built edifice, in the Byzantine style, and highly effective in its architectural features. This building, when completed, will be used as the landing-place for passengers from the European steamers and the reception of their baggage pending examination. The inconvenience and discomfort to which travelers have been exposed in the past will thus be obviated. The barge-office will also be the headquarters of the various boats used in the revenue service. The old barge-office at No. 6 State Street has long been inadequate to the rapidly expanding needs of the Custom-House, and the convenience of this important branch of the Government service is much benefited by the new building. The different branches of the customs department of New York have been widely scattered, owing to insufficient accommodation, and public necessity will ere long compel the erection of an edifice by the United States Government, which will embrace these divisions as far as possible under one roof.

Passing from the buildings devoted to government uses to those belonging to corporations

Grand Central Depot.

4

Columbia College. (New building.)

and educational institutions, that which first singles itself out for notice is the Grand Central Depot, the terminal station of the New York Central, the Harlem, and the New Haven Railways. It is the only large railway-depot in the precincts of New York, with the exception of the old Hudson River Railroad Station on Thirtieth Street and Tenth Avenue, now used for suburban trains only. The exterior is imposing, and the immense size and regularity give it a marked prominence, notwithstanding the simplicity of the architectural features, its massive plainness being well suited to its purposes. Approaching from Fifth Avenue, the eye is first caught by the great towers and then by the main or western façade. The situation of this great headquarters of the railway interest is between Fourth or Park Avenue and Vanderbilt Avenue, and extends from Forty-second to Forty-fifth Street.

The external walls are built of red brick with white trimmings. The offices of the three railways which terminate here are on the west and south sides, there being three stories on the west and five on the south, including the Mansard roof and domes. The space for trains is covered by a glass and iron roof, having a single arch of a span of two hundred feet, and an altitude of one hundred and ten feet. The traveler, as he steps off a train on the stone platform and casts his eye upward, can have but one sentiment, that of unmingled admiration for the skill which has spanned three acres with one magnificent arched roof. The total length of the building is six hundred and ninety-five feet, which is also the length of the glass roof, and its width two hundred and forty feet. Twelve trains, consisting of twelve cars and a locomotive each, can be admitted into the great car-house at once, standing side by side on the parallel tracks.

Astor Library.

Besides the various offices, passenger waiting-rooms, and baggage-rooms, there are a police-station, a lunch-room, and a barber's shop in the basement. About one hundred and twenty-five trains arrive and depart daily, but everything is done with such thorough system that crowding or confusion is a thing almost unknown.

The oldest and most important of the collegiate institutions in New York is Columbia, first chartered in 1754 as King's College. It now ranks among the very first colleges of the coun-

Lenox Library.

try, coming next after Yale and Harvard in reputation, wealth of endowment, and extended facilities for scholastic training. Previous to the year in which it was chartered, a fund of about thirty-eight hundred pounds was raised in England, to be applied to the founding of such an institution, and out of that fund the first expenses of the college were met. Even after the granting of the charter the college had a hard struggle for existence, the predominance of the Church of England, or Episcopal, element in its board of governors having awakened the jealousy of the other religious denominations. The Trinity Church vestry-room was used for recita-

Normal College

tions for several years, and the corporation of that church finally set the college firmly on its feet by granting it a portion of the church lands. These lands were between what is now called College Place and Mercer Street, and here the first college building was erected. At the outbreak of the War of the Revolution in 1776 the college was looked upon as a hot-bed of Toryism, and consequently the Committee of Public Safety resolved on breaking it up by directing its officers to prepare the buildings for the reception of troops. From this time until 1784, when the Legislature of the State reincorporated it under its present name, the college was in abeyance, so to speak. The library had been scattered and the buildings were in ruins, so that the regents, the new governing body, had almost to recreate the institution. The new charter proving defective, it was amended in 1787, so that the management of the college was vested in a self-perpetuating body of twenty-four trustees, and this body has existed to the present time.

About 1850 the old buildings on College Place were found to be too far down town, and the present site, on Forty-ninth and Fiftieth Streets and Madison and Fourth Avenues, was selected.

When the new buildings shall have been entirely constructed on the plan projected, they will make a noble home for a great and time-honored institution. There are four departments connected with Columbia College—the academic, the scientific, the legal, and the medical—the latter being better known as the College of Physicians and Surgeons. There are no halls whatever connected with or attached to the college, the students being supposed to reside with their relatives or some private family. The corps of professors numbers about sixty, and the income is derived mainly from the rentals of the real estate granted to the college by Trinity Church.

The Astor Library must be ranked as the largest and finest collection of books for the general uses of the scholar in New York, though the Lenox has more rare special works. The building is located in Lafayette Place, and is a handsome and massive pile of brick and brownstone, in the Romanesque style of architecture. The first endowment was by John Jacob Astor, some thirty years ago, to the amount of four hundred thousand dollars, which was supplemented by his son, William B. Astor. The property of the library at the present time in building, books, and funds, amounts to more than one million dollars. Important improvements are now being made by the generosity of John Jacob Astor, the present representative of the family, who in 1879 deeded to the institution three adjacent lots, making seventy-five feet front by one hundred and fifty deep. On this has been recently erected an addition, sixty-five feet wide by one hundred deep, in the same general style as the rest of the building. The total effect is shown in the illustration. The additional library space will give accommodation to one hundred and twenty thousand more volumes, a highly desirable expansion, as the library has for some time been seriously embarrassed for room.

The library as now constituted is divided into the Hall of Sciences and Hall of Histories, the latter including everything in the way of miscellaneous literature. Above the main reading-rooms there are sixty alcoves, and the volumes now on

St. Joseph's Home, Lafayette Place.

the shelves very nearly approach two hundred thousand, which can only be used on the premises for reference purposes. Any respectable person may have access to the treasures of the institution, and the librarian and assistants are always willing to assist the student by suggestions in the investigation of any study. Permission to use the alcoves for study and work may also be obtained, if satisfactory references are brought. Although some of the departments are deficient, the Astor library, on the whole, may be pronounced to be remarkably well equipped for the working needs of the scholar. The average yearly attendance for some years past has been about sixty thousand readers. Among the treasures in the library are a number of very rich and rare manuscripts in Greek and Latin, given by Mr. Astor. It has the largest manuscript volume known; it is the volume of chants used at the coronation of the French kings for many years, and is superbly illuminated with vignettes by well-known early French artists. These books will be shown by the librarian on application. A number of black-letter works, including a copy of the first printed Bible, are also in the library, and a fair collection of Shakespeareana.

During the past year the United States Sanitary Commission deposited in the Astor Library the archives of the commission, and, after a career of eighteen years, ceased to exist. These records of the most complete and effective work in relieving the

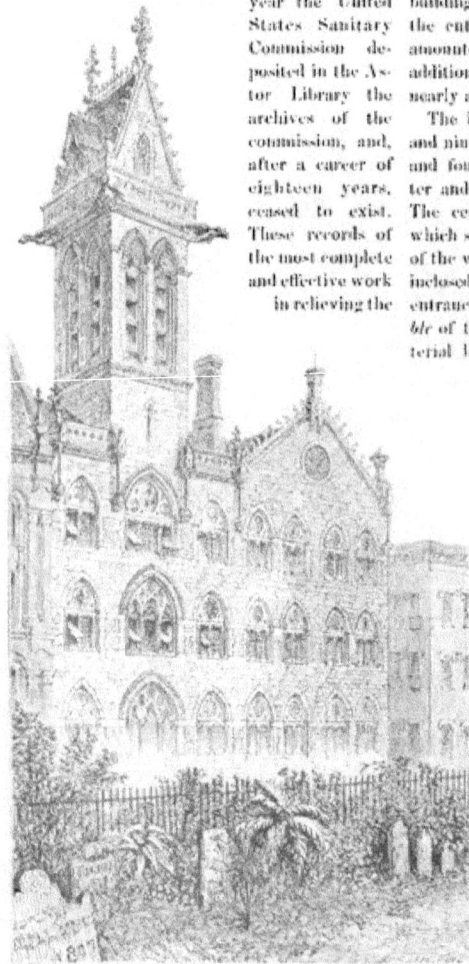
Trinity-Parish School.

sorrows and sufferings of war which the world had up to that time seen, are a very valuable monument to the zeal and intelligence of the American people, and form an important part of the unwritten history of the great civil war.

The only rival to the Astor, the Lenox Library, is opposite the east side of Central Park, in Fifth Avenue, between Seventieth and Seventy-first Streets. This gift to New York was the culmination of a long series of benefactions which the city owes to the late James Lenox, one of its wealthiest citizens, and most indefatigable collectors of literary and art treasures. The present building was first opened to visitors in 1877, and the entire cost of construction and furnishing amounted to more than a million dollars. In addition to this there is a permanent fund of nearly a quarter of a million dollars.

The building has a frontage of one hundred and ninety-two feet and a depth of one hundred and fourteen feet. The arrangement is a center and two wings, facing west on the avenue. The center has a façade of ninety-two feet, which stands back forty-two feet from the front of the wings, thus making a courtyard, which is inclosed by a massive iron railing. The public entrance is through this courtyard. The *ensemble* of the building is solid and striking, the material being of a light-colored limestone. The wings are divided into two stories each, and arranged for library and reading-rooms, the size being one hundred and eight by three hundred feet. The south wing is devoted to the less valuable books, and contains shelf-room for one hundred thousand volumes, while the north wing is set apart for rare books, too precious for ordinary handling.

The picture-gallery is in the central part of the second story, and contains about one hundred and fifty canvases by artists principally modern, but including many noted names.

Of the books in the collection a very large number are *incunabula*, or specimens of the first products of the typographic art—first editions, Bibles, Shakespeareana, and Americana. There are also copies of every known edition of Walton's "Angler," of Bunyan's "Pilgrim's Progress," and of nearly every known edition of Milton. In illustrated works, and in works on the fine arts generally, the library is also very complete. It is rich in rare MSS., including illustrated Bibles on vellum and paper, belonging to the four centuries immediately preceding the Reformation. There are at present about thirty thousand volumes. In addition to the works of art already mentioned, there are many carvings, works of statuary, *bric-à-brac*, and keramics. It is a pity that this fine museum of literary and art wealth should be practically sealed to the public by vexatious restrictions, the condition of admission being the procuring of a ticket from the superintendent on the day before.

An institution of which New York is justly proud—for it is the finest of its kind in America—is the Normal College, which occupies a site in Sixty-ninth Street, between Fourth and Lexington Avenues. The building is spacious and massive, and after the ecclesiastical model. The college building proper is about three hundred feet long, one hundred and twenty-five feet wide, facing Fourth Avenue, seventy-eight feet wide in the rear, and over seventy feet high. It is of the Gothic style, and has a lofty Victoria tower. The college is a part of the common-school sys-

New York Hospital, West Fifteenth Street, between Fifth and Sixth Avenues.

tem, and is under the control of the Board of Education, the ostensible object being to prepare young women to teach, though but few of the graduates follow the profession.

The college contains thirty recitation-rooms, three large lecture-rooms, a calisthenium, a library, six retiring-rooms for instructors, president's offices, and a main hall, capable of seating sixteen hundred students. Each recitation-room contains seats for forty-eight, and each lecture room for one hundred and forty-four persons. The entire cost of the building was three hundred and fifty thousand dollars. A model or

training school is erected in the rear, in which pupil-teachers have an opportunity to supplement their theoretic studies with the practical. About sixteen hundred pupils are usually registered on the college books, and the course of study includes Latin, physics, chemistry, German, natural science, French, drawing, and music. It costs the city about one hundred thousand dollars a year to maintain this fine institution. The discipline is said to be very strict and the control over the army of young women daily assembled of the most perfect order.

Among the many charitable institutions erected and controlled by the Roman Catholic Church, St. Joseph's Home, at the corner of Lafayette Place and Great Jones Street, is noteworthy. Built by St. Joseph's Union for newsboys, bootblacks, and similar waifs and strays, it is designed to furnish this large class what shall be at once a home, a school, and religious training. The building will contain extensive schoolrooms, a chapel, library, dormitories, refection-rooms, etc. The dimensions are one hundred and eighty by eighty feet, with a height of ten stories, including Mansard roof and basement. This edifice is made as near fire-proof as possible, window-casings and door-frames being the only wood used, and all the rest of the interior fittings being of slate and marble. The administration and discipline of the institution will be of the most thorough character. The total cost of St. Joseph's Home is estimated at nearly one hundred and fifty thousand dollars.

Another religious educational school of much interest in its denominational connection is that of Trinity parish, situated on New Church Street, nearly opposite the rear of Trinity Church. It is a handsome brown-stone structure of modern Gothic architecture, and is exclusively devoted

Roosevelt Hospital, Ninth Avenue and Fifty-ninth Street.

to parochial interests. The school is for boys only, and is maintained at an outlay of six thousand dollars annually. The scholars are taught all the English branches, Latin, French, German, and instrumental music. There are no charges whatever, and the attendance is about three hundred.

New York is specially rich in hospitals, some being purely public institutions, and others under the control of religious denominations. Altogether there are thirty-nine of these beneficent asylums for the sick and needy, many of them having also special accommodations for paying patients. In most cases these institutions have attained a degree of excellence in management and comfort in appointments which render them more desirable as refuges during illness than almost any private house or home. This is especially the case with the New York, St. Luke's, and Roosevelt Hospitals, where by paying a small amount the best medical attendance and nursing can be had.

First among these great hospitals let us note the New York, which is located in Fifteenth Street, between Fifth and Sixth Avenues. This palatial building, with its countless windows and wide balconies, is a commanding object of attention. The material used is red brick with stone and iron facings. The hospital is more than a century old, and the corporation is immensely rich. The present building was opened in the spring of 1876, and its interior is furnished sumptuously. Some of the rooms for private patients are let at forty dollars a week, but the charge for patients in the wards is only seven dollars a week, while the deserving poor are cared for gratuitously. In one of the upper stories there is a solarium, roofed in with glass and furnished with

Mount Sinai Hospital. Sixty-sixth Street.

easy lounges, masses of flowers, shrubs, and aquaria. The dullest day is cheerful in this paradise, and the entire building is arranged so as to form a snare for sunbeams. The dietary is liberal, the nurses are attentive, and the medical staff includes well-known physicians and surgeons. An ambulance service is connected with the institution, and all street accidents are brought in regardless of the sufferers' ability to pay.

Separate apartments for the nurses, dining-rooms, and lavatories are placed at the end of each ward, and each of the six stories is connected with the others by two large elevators. All the cooking and laundry-work is done at the top of the building, from the rest of which all disagreeable odors are thus excluded.

Another admirable institution of this kind is the Roosevelt Hospital, endowed by the late James Roosevelt, situated at the corner of Fifty-

The Lenox Hospital.

ninth Street and Ninth Avenue. The edifice is built on the pavilion plan, and the style of architecture is the modern secular Gothic. There are accommodations for one hundred and eighty patients, and many of the beds are owned by private individuals, this privilege being purchased for three thousand dollars, and carrying with it the right to send one patient at a time to the hospital. The splendid accommodations of this hospital are surpassed by none in the city.

The Mount Sinai Hospital, which is under the control of the Hebrew denomination, is in Lexington Avenue, between Sixty-sixth and Sixty-seventh Streets. The buildings are of the Elizabethan style of architecture, and are faced with brick and marble trimmings. It

Masonic Temple, on Twenty-third Street and Sixth Avenue.

accommodates one hundred and sixty patients. It is very complete, and embodies all the improvements of modern art in its interior arrangements for the comfort of patients.

Prominent among public and private edifices, which rise in towers, domes, and stately proportions, may be observed the imposing façade of another noble hospital charity, the Lenox Hospital, endowed by the will of the late James Lenox. It consists of a central building and two extensive wings of a corresponding character, one of which is partly shown in the illustration, and is situated in Seventieth Street. The hospital has also very extensive and complete accommodations, and ranks among the most important of the numerous benefactions of its founder. These are but a few

Booth's Theatre, corner of Twenty-third Street and Sixth Avenue.

BUILDINGS. 59

of the charitable institutions for the sick in New York, free admission and attendance being in all cases given to the poor, though such as are able to pay are expected to do so according to their means and the luxury of the surroundings furnished. In all essential ways, however, the care of the pauper is just as efficient as that of the wealthiest patient.

One of the finest buildings in New York is the Masonic Temple, at the northeast corner of Sixth Avenue and Twenty-third Street. Its material is granite, and it displays a breadth of treatment in its various parts, a severe and classical style in its ornamentation, which strongly commends it to all lovers of good taste in archi-

The Grand Opera-House, corner of Twenty-third Street and Eighth Avenue.

tecture. The main entrance, in Twenty-third Street, is through a Doric portico of coupled

Seventh Regiment Armory.

Doric columns. The first story is devoted to business purposes. The next story is treated in the Ionic style, and devoted to the use of the Grand Lodge and its officials. When this body is not in session, however, the grand hall is rented for lectures and concerts. The third and fourth stories are occupied exclusively by lodge and chapter rooms. The Mansard story is used by the Knight Templars, and is the most complete commandery, in all its arrangements, in existence. It may be of interest to state that the first subscription toward the erection of the building was made by the great tragedian, Edwin Forrest, and that the fund in a few years amounted to more than the needed sum. The outlay of money reached more than a million dollars. The net rental is devoted entirely to the support of the widows and orphans of Masons.

On the same side of Sixth Avenue, and im-

Union League Club.

mediately opposite the Masonic Temple, is the most notable of the structures in New York devoted to the drama, the splendid theatre built by Edwin Booth, eleven years ago, as a home for tragedy. It is a truly noble edifice, of Concord granite, in the style of the Renaissance. The dimensions are one hundred and forty-nine feet in length and ninety feet in height, including a Mansard roof of twenty-four feet. The auditorium seats about two thousand people, and is one of the most beautiful in its lines and decoration in the world. It has three galleries, and, in spite of some unfortunate changes in its interior arrangements made by Mr. Dion Boucicault, still remains the most attractive of the New York theatres. It is one of the very few theatres where every part of the stage can be easily seen from every seat in the house.

Mr. Booth filled his high ambition of giving the finest performances of tragedy which could be put on the stage in respect of acting, stage setting, and general surroundings, for a few years, but at such ultimate loss to himself that he was finally obliged to yield up possession of his theatre, a catastrophe precipitated by the load of debt which had been incurred in completing the very costly structure. During the Booth *régime*

the Shakespearean tragedies were produced with a splendor which made the theatre the talk of the country, and could only be compared with that notable revival by Charles Kean in London, a quarter of a century since, considered by the English critics as one of the landmarks in the history of the modern English stage. After its failure in Booth's hands, the property was sold, and since that time has been leased by a

"The Victoria."

succession of managers, who have presented melodrama, pantomime, spectacles, comedy, etc. One interesting feature of this theatre is the facility of exit, possible in case of fire or other exigency. Seven doors on the Twenty-third Street side, leading directly from the auditorium, can be thrown open at once, and the theatre be emptied in less than two minutes.

Two squares westward from Booth's Theatre,

in Twenty-third Street, stands another fine temple of amusement, the Grand Opera-House, at the corner of Eighth Avenue. This is a massive edifice of white marble, erected by the Western speculator, Pike, more than a dozen years since. It has a front of one hundred and thirteen feet on Eighth Avenue, and ninety-eight feet on Twenty-third Street. The theatre proper is a rear building, the approach to which is through

"The Florence."

a spacious vestibule from each street. Failing as a theatre from the very start, it was purchased by James Fisk and Jay Gould, and the upper stories occupied by the Erie Railway offices until after the death of Fisk. A significant fact in the history of this place of amusement, and one well worth noticing, is that, after having been a permanent failure at high prices, it was opened by managers who were shrewd enough to see the immense clientage which New York afforded for good performances at moderate rates. Since that time the Grand Opera-House has been a successful institution, and has given the public a class of entertainments fully up to the general average of the dramatic art, but at popular prices.

The most noticeable building of its kind in New York is the new armory built for the Seventh Regiment, occupying a complete block, between Sixty-sixth and Sixty-seventh Streets, and Fourth and Lexington Avenues, covering a site two hundred feet by four hundred and five. Facing Fourth Avenue is the administration building, which occupies the whole frontage, and leaves the remaining two hundred by three hundred feet for a drill-room. There are ten company drill-rooms, a board of officers' room, a veterans' room, a reading-room, a reception-room, a field and staff room, a gymnasium, and six squad drill-rooms. The material is Philadelphia brick, with granite trimmings, and the cost of it was more than three hundred thousand dollars. The interior was decorated, fitted, and furnished at the expense of the regiment and the contributions of the public, and the armory may justly be called a magnificent club-house, as well as the most complete hall of military exercise in the country.

Among the splendid buildings recently erected in New York, the new home of the Union League Club, on the corner of Fifth Avenue and Thirty-ninth Street, is one of the most noticeable. The architecture is composite, various styles being harmonized to make a very picturesque exterior. It was built and decorated at an expense of about four hundred thousand dollars. The building was expressly designed for the requirements of a club-house, and is probably the most complete structure of the kind in America. On the first floor it contains a large and well-appointed reading and conversation room, billiard-room, and café. On the second floor, extending the length of the Fifth Avenue front, is the library, a beautiful and richly decorated room, containing a collection of about three thousand volumes. An admirable arrangement of the bookcases furnishes many a cozy nook for the quiet reader. The eastern half of the second floor is devoted to the art-gallery and general meeting-room of the club. The dining-room, in many respects the most notable apartment in the building, is heavily paneled with oak, and the high, vaulted ceiling is decorated from designs by Mr. John La Farge, of Boston. The general decoration of the halls, gallery, meeting-room, private dining-room, and other parts of the house, is executed from designs by Louis Tiffany, of New York, and Franklin Smith, of Boston.

In Twenty-seventh Street, extending from Fifth Avenue to Broadway, is the fine structure formerly known as the Stevens House, but now as the Victoria Hotel. It was built by the late Mr. Paran Stevens, the well-known hotel-keeper, as a model example of an apartment-house, where wealthy families might enjoy all the pleasures and comforts of housekeeping with a minimum of its vexations. It has recently been transformed into an hotel, though it appears to

Park Avenue Hotel.

have been highly successful in its adaptation to the original purpose.

Perhaps the finest specimen of the palatial apartment-house now to be seen in New York is the Florence, a superb edifice in Eighteenth Street, at the northeast corner of Fourth Avenue. The rents of suites in this building are very high, and are only within the reach of the wealthy. For sumptuousness and completeness of appointments, the Florence is a model, as the most lavish expenditure of money was united with all the results of skill and experience in its building.

Another noble edifice may be seen at the corner of Park Avenue and Thirty-third Street,

built by the late A. T. Stewart, and opened with great éclat in the spring of 1878, as a Woman's Hotel. It is an iron structure of immense size and profuse ornamentation, and designed to be fire-proof. This quondam charity proposed to furnish a home for the better class of working-women at rates within their means, but the experiment was found to be practically a failure, whether the fault was inherent in the design itself or in the practical management, and after a few months of trial it was opened as an hotel of the established pattern, under the name of the Park Avenue Hotel.

Returning again to down-town New York, let us take a brief glance at several remarkable buildings previously overlooked. At the corner of Dey Street and Broadway, the Western Union Telegraph Company have erected a noble edifice for their offices. It is eight stories high, and is built of pressed red brick, granite, and marble. Above the roof, which is higher than its neighbors, there is a clock-tower, and from nearly every window threads of fine wire issue, connecting every important center of population, festooning every great post-road, marking the black track of every railway, and, in fact, literally blending town, city, country, ocean, and river. Could we see the inside of the operating-room, our pulses would beat a stroke faster in sympathy with the activity of its denizens.

"A hundred keys and sounders," a writer has said, "are clicking at once, making a noise like a diminutive cotton-mill. The floor is filled with ranges of tables, at which the operators are seated, separated from each other by glass screens.

Western Union Company's Telegraph-Building.

Against one wall is the switch-board, the most conspicuous object in the room. Without any actual resemblance, it recalls to the imaginations of many of the visitors the thought of a great organ, its ranges of slender wires behind the screen suggesting the trackers and pipes and the innumerable switches representing the keys and stops. Boys are passing to and fro with papers, and messages are being sent and received from almost every table in the room. The switch-board is the central ganglion of the whole system. Every current passes through this apparatus. The manager, standing here, can, by inserting a brass wedge in the course of any current, hear what message is passing. He has thus the means of inspecting and listening

marks the place. The old drab building of the "Tribune," for a long time one of the landmarks of journalism, has been supplanted by a new structure, finished in its present state about four years ago, but still incomplete so far as affects the whole plan. This new structure is one of the largest and handsomest newspaper offices in the world. Its style is composite, and it is constructed of red pressed brick, granite, marble, and iron. It is one story higher than the Western Union Telegraph Office, and is the highest building on Manhattan Island. Above the nine stories there is a lofty clock-tower, visible from all points around the city, than which the "Tribune Association" could not have erected a more suit-

The "Tribune" and "Times" Buildings, Printing-House Square.

to all that is going on over all the wires connected with the office."

Passing the City Hall Park we enter what is known as Printing-House Square, from the fact that the principal newspaper buildings of New York, including the "Times," "Tribune," "Sun," "World," and "Staats-Zeitung," are there located. A bronze statue of Benjamin Franklin, erected under the auspices of Captain Benjamin De Groot in 1871, also appropriately

able monument to the advancing power of journalism.

A few squares up Broadway we reach the imposing building of the New York Life Insurance Company at the corner of Leonard Street, one of the finest ever erected by private enterprise in America. It is of pure white marble, of the Ionic order of architecture, the design having been suggested by the temple of Erectheus at Athens. The exterior is a model of

5

New York Life-Insurance Building.

architectural taste, and the offices within are remarkable for beauty and convenience. The appointments of the interior are very handsome and tasteful. The company is one of the oldest in the country. We give here also a view of the establishment of A. T. Stewart & Co., in Broadway, between Ninth and Tenth Streets, probably the most extensive trade palace in the world.

A. T. Stewart & Co.'s, Broadway, from Ninth to Tenth Street.

CHURCHES.

THE ecclesiastical edifices of New York are worthy of the greatness of the city in number, size, and architectural beauty. The principal denominations seem to have vied with each other in erecting noble churches, and in no direction have the wealth and public spirit of the citizens of the metropolis shown themselves more efficiently. First among the temples of religion which are specially noticeable must be mentioned Trinity, the principal church of Trinity Parish, a corporation closely woven with the history of New York, and remarkable for the extent of its charities, and the important part it plays in the denominational interest of the Protestant Episcopal Church of America.

Standing at the head of Wall Street in Broadway, it is certainly one of the most cathedral-like and elegant structures in the country. Its position, right in the thick of the business traffic, which beats against its very walls and reverberates with a roar like that of the ocean-surf, gives the location a peculiar interest and suggestiveness; and when the mellow chimes ring out their rich music over the struggle of the worldly battle below, the reflective bystander can hardly help a rush of strange thoughts. Before describing the church, let us briefly glance at the history of the church organiza-

Trinity Church and Martyrs' Monument

tion, which is the oldest and richest in the United States.

The land on which Trinity Church now stands was granted by the English Government in 1697, being in the fifth year of the reign of William and Mary, the location being fixed as "in or near to a street without the North Gate of the city, commonly called Broadway." Eight years later, in 1705, the entire tract between Vesey and Christopher Streets along the North River, known as "Queen Anne's Farm," was presented to the church from the same source. A large portion of this magnificent endowment is still controlled by the organization, but for many years parts of it were bestowed with a liberal hand on all sorts of institutions that could present a plausible claim for assistance. The landed property of Trinity is popularly supposed to be something enormous, and so it appears when figured out at building-lot prices. When estimated, however, by the income derived from it, the total is not so very startling, being only about half a million dollars per annum. This amount goes to the maintenance of the parish church and six chapels, and a multitude of charities connected with them, and to keeping alive about a dozen other churches in the poorer quarters in the city. The first church was completed in 1697, and stood unchanged for forty years, when it was almost rebuilt. At the outbreak of the Revolution it was closed for a time, owing to the persistence of the clergy in reading the prayers for the King of England. When the British army had established itself again firmly in the city, the doors were again opened, but after a few days it was destroyed in the great fire of 1776, which consumed four hundred and ninety-three houses. It was not rebuilt until twelve years had elapsed, the congregation worshiping in the mean time in St. Paul's Chapel. The structure then erected stood until 1839, when it was pronounced unsafe, and pulled down to make way for the present one, which was finished in 1846.

This is still one of the handsomest specimens of Gothic church architecture in the city, and its right to rank as the most conspicuous structure of the lower part of the city has not yet been taken away by the many stately public and corporate buildings that have been reared in the neighborhood since its dedication. Looking up from Wall Street we see its steeple rising to a height of two hundred and eighty-four feet, conveying an impression of size which buildings of greater dimensions but less fortunately situated do not give. The material used—a

St. Paul's Chapel—View from Graveyard.

brown sandstone—also helps to increase the general effect, offering as it does a decided contrast to the marble and granite of this financial quarter, on the ears of whose denizens the famous church chimes break with refreshing sweetness. The doors are generally open in the daytime, and nowhere else probably can a more striking change of surroundings be produced in a few seconds than by walking during business hours from the mercenary uproar of the Stock Exchange, only a few yards distant, through these doors. The stillness is only broken by the hushed and apparently distant rumbling of the incessant traffic in Broadway and the chirruping of the English sparrows, dwellers of the trees in the churchyard. The gray tint of the groined roof and its supporting rows of carved Gothic columns is mellowed by the subdued daylight, which is warmed and toned in its passage through the richly stained windows, while the altar and reredos rise with their picturesque alternations of color wherein red and white predominate, and form an artistic *ensemble* well worthy of contemplation.

This altar and reredos were built to the memory of the late William B. Astor by his two sons, the reredos occupying nearly the whole width of the chancel, and being carried up some twenty feet from the floor. The altar is eleven feet long, and is constructed of pure white statuary marble, with shafts of Lisbon red marble supporting capitals carved in natural foliage, dividing the front and side into panels. In the central panel, which is carved with passion-flowers, is a Maltese cross in mosaic, set with cameos; a head of Christ, and the symbols of the Evangelists. Two kneeling angels flank it. The other panels are carved with ears of wheat, also in mosaic. The white-marble slab is set on a cornice composed of grape-vines, and is inlaid with five crosses of red marble. The super-altar is of red Lisbon marble with the words "Holy, Holy, Holy" in mosaics on its face, and its shelf is continued on each side the whole length of the reredos for the reception of flowers at festivals. The design of the reredos is perpendicular Gothic, and the material is Caen-stone elaborately carved after natural foliage. In the lower portion, on each side of the altar, are three

Grace Church, corner of Broadway and Tenth Street.

square panels filled with colored mosaics in geo-
metrical patterns; and above the line of the
super-altar are seven panels of white marble,
sculptured in *alto-rilievo*, representing incidents
in the life of Christ immediately preceding and
subsequent to the last supper. The reredos is
divided into three bays by buttresses with various religious representations in them, including
statuettes of the twelve apostles. Both the altar
and the reredos are exceedingly beautiful, and
add much to the interest of grand old Trinity,
which has always been an attraction to visitors.

A variety of charities are connected with the
church, including the Trinity Infirmary for the
sick poor of the parish; five beds at St. Luke's
Hospital; a burial-place for the poor, and a
burial-place for the cler-
gy. There are also five
scholarships in Trinity
College, Hartford, the

holders of which are relieved from all term
bills, fees, and charges during their college
course.

In the ancient churchyard are to be seen
many memorials of interest. Here reposes the
body of Alexander Hamilton, slain by Burr in
the celebrated duel; and here, close at hand, is
the tomb of Captain Lawrence, whose dying
words, as he lay on the bloody deck of the Ches-
apeake, "Don't give up the ship!" are familiar
to every American schoolboy. There is also a
beautiful brown-stone monument, built by the
Trinity Corporation, in memory of "Patriotic
Americans who died during the Revolution in
British prisons." This was done at a time when
it was proposed to extend Pine Street along the
line on which it now stands, and has generally
been regarded as a diplomatic move to prevent
the desecration of the old churchyard. No one
should visit the church without inspecting the
graveyard, for here are to be seen many venerable moss-covered stones, with their ancient in-
scriptions, some of them very quaint and curious, the connecting links between the
living and the dead.

The chapels of Trinity, most of
them fine churches in themselves, are
St. Paul's, St. John's, Trinity Chapel,
St. Chrysostom's, St. Augustine's, and
St. Cornelius's, the last being on Governor's Island in the harbor, and devoted to the use of the military chapel.
Most of the churches of the parish are
free, or nearly so, the exception being
pews, which belong to old families, and
have been held for generations.

St. Paul's is as well known to the
New-Yorker as the parent edifice. It
was the third church built in the city,
the first being Trinity, the second St.
George's, which stood at the corner of
Beekman and Cliff Streets, and was
also built by the Trinity Corporation,
though the present St. George's in
Rutherford Place is an independent
organization.

The corner-stone of St. Paul's was
laid in 1764, and it was finished two
years later. When this church was
built, the frontage toward the North
River was regarded as superior to that
on Broadway. So the rear of the edifice now faces the great artery of New
York life and traffic. The position of
the church is between Fulton and
Vesey Streets, and the casual spectator

St. Augustine Chapel. East Houston Street.

St. Patrick's Cathedral, Fifth Avenue.

is for a time perplexed as he notices the tower on the rear of the church, and the massive porch and pillars denoting the main entrance, accessible only through the churchyard on the side. Perhaps this irregularity adds to the sense of antiquity and strangeness which one inevitably feels in looking through the iron fence into the solemn old graveyard, with its moldy and time-eaten tombs.

St. Paul's, as it now stands, is the oldest church edifice in the city, the original Trinity Church having been destroyed after its erection, and the yard around it adds to its venerable associations. In the rear wall facing Broadway is a memorial tablet to General Richard Montgomery, who fell in battle in the ill-fated Quebec expedition during the Revolutionary War; while in the churchyard are monuments to Thomas Addis Emmet, the Irish patriot, George Frederick Cooke, the celebrated English actor, and others. The monument to Cooke was built at the expense of the great Edmund Kean, when that actor, who had an unbounded admiration of Cooke, was in this country; and it was afterward successively restored by Charles Kean and Edward Sothern, the well-known comedian who recently died. This most quaint and interesting spot, with its ancient tombs bearing names of the foremost old New York families, is well worth a visit by those who have any antiquarian sympathies, or who would seclude themselves for a short time in a place only a few feet from the fevered life of the street, and bury themselves in the silent recollections of the past. It is interesting to note that many old families residing far up-town still, by force of long association, attend service at this ancient shrine.

St. Augustine's Chapel, another of the edifices connected with Trinity Parish, is in Houston Street, just east of the Bowery. It was finished in 1877, and is one of the most complete and pretty little churches in New York. It is built of brown-stone, in the Gothic style, and contains schoolrooms as well as a chapel. The steeple bears at its summit a crystal cross, which on Sunday and feast-day nights is illumined by gas-jets placed within it, so that it is seen shining out clearly against the sky for some distance away. The interior is of the Queen Anne style, and is well worth a visit as the best specimen of the kind in New York. The entrance from the street is through a broad archway, with ornamental iron gates opening into a spacious passage-way, with an encaustic-tile pavement and timbered ceiling. The walls are built of neutral-tinted brick, with bands of terra-cotta tiles underneath the brackets, carrying the ash beams of the paneled ceiling. A low round arch at the end, with glass doors, forms the entrance to the chapel vestibule. The chapel is a mass of rich color, caused by the combination of mahogany rafters, ornamental walls and ceilings, polished brass gas-fixtures, butternut-wood

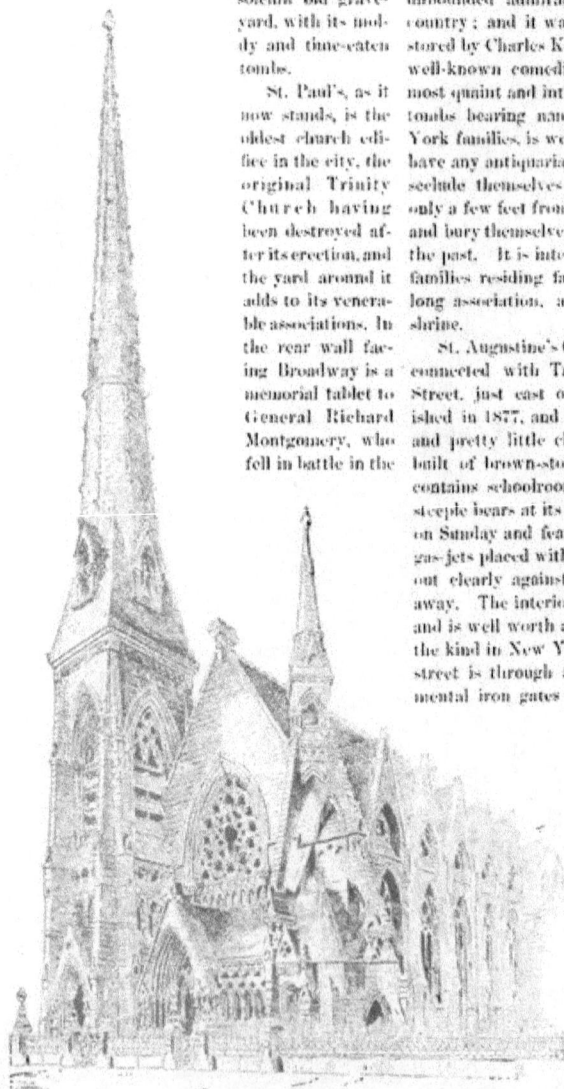

Reformed Dutch Church, Fifth Avenue and Forty-Mth Street.

pews, etc.; and the effect is of the most pleasing kind. The ground occupied by the entire building, of which the chapel occupies the rear only, is eighty-six feet wide in front and one hundred and fifty in the rear, with a depth of two hundred and eighty feet. The schools and mission-rooms are also handsomely furnished, and worthy of a visit. The surrounding district is very poor, and this beautiful chapel is the only Episcopal place of worship for quite a distance, thus filling a most important religious function in this portion of the city. Perhaps the greatest value of Trinity Parish as an organization is this genuine service for the wants of the poor.

Grace Church, at the corner of Tenth Street and Broadway, is, after Trinity, the richest parish in New York, and, as may be fancied, is one of the most fashionable places of worship. It has been the scene of more aristocratic weddings and funerals than any other place of worship. The bridal parties that the celebrated sexton, Brown, who

Church, corner of Lexington Avenue and Sixty-third Street.

died about a year ago, ushered into its sacred precincts during his long career, would cover a catalogue of the most distinguished family names in New York. The present structure was erected in 1845, and is one of the finest churches in the city, the material being of white granite, and the style a chaste but yet ornamental Gothic. Its position is probably the best in the city, considered from an architectural point of view, standing as it does just where Broadway leaves its direct northern course and takes a sudden turn to the northwest, so that the porch and the steeple completely close the view from the south. The parsonage of the church is similar in design, adjoins the church-building on the north, and stands back from the busy street. Adjoining the church on the south stands a small addition, in design and material like the church, which is used for daily services, and is called the chantry. The funds necessary for its erection were furnished by Miss Catherine Wolff. A new building, connecting the church with the rectory, was

Synagogue, Lexington Avenue and F fty fifth Street.

erected in 1880, and is used as a study, vestry-room, etc.

It is not, however, in the exterior, attractive as this may be, that the visitor to New York will find the most pleasure. There is a positive æsthetic pleasure to be derived from the simple and yet luxurious and rich interior of the building, which is flooded on fine days with the light filtered through the stained-glass windows. The music is among the very best in the city, as the choir is made up of distinguished vocalists, and there are two organs, connected by electricity, which the organist can use together. The rector,

Rev. Dr. Potter, is one of the most eloquent and effective preachers in New York. On a fine Sunday morning one may see perhaps a more splendid parade of the wealth and fashion of the city than is gathered within the walls of any other church.

The finest and most imposing church-building, not only in New York, but in the New World, is the new St. Patrick's Cathedral, which, although the spires are yet unfinished, is a magnificent specimen of Gothic architecture. It occupies the most elevated site in Fifth Avenue, extending the entire front of the block on the east side, between Fiftieth and Fifty-first Streets, and running back to Madison Avenue. When the Chapel of Our Lady, which is included in the design, is completed, the building will cover the whole square.

This grand Roman Catholic Cathedral has now been building for twenty-three years, and it will probably not be fully finished in all the details of its design for several years to come. It was projected by Archbishop Hughes, in 1850, and the plans were soon afterward drawn by James Renwick. The corner-stone was laid in the presence of a hundred thousand people, on August 15, 1858. At that time very few of the fine residences which now line Fifth Avenue for miles above the cathedral had been built, and there was no house to be seen from Fifth to Sixth Avenue. The architecture of the cathedral is of the decorated or geometric style that prevailed in Europe in the thirteenth century, of which the Cathedrals of Rheims, Cologne, and Amiens on the Continent, and the naves of York Minster, Exeter, and Westminster, are fine exponents. The ground-plan is in the form of a Latin cross, and the dimensions are: interior length, three hundred and six feet; breadth of nave and choir, ninety-six feet, without the chapels, and one hundred and twenty feet with the chapels; length of the transept, one hundred and forty feet; height, one hundred and eight feet; height of side-aisles, fifty-four feet. The Fifth Avenue front consists of a central gable, one hundred and fifty-six feet in height, with towers and spires each three hundred and thirty feet in height; but at present the towers reach only to the roof. The design of the grand portal also contemplates the statues of the twelve apostles to be placed within it, but this has not yet been done. The building is of white marble, with a base-course of granite. The interior of the cathedral is as fine as its exterior. The massive columns which support the roof are of white stone, thirty-five feet in height, and clustered, having a combined diameter of five feet. The ceiling is groined, with richly-molded ribs and foliage-bosses. The springing line of the ceiling is seventy-seven feet from the floor. The organ-gallery, in the nave between the towers, is forty-six feet wide and twenty-eight feet long, and is built of ash, with richly-molded front and ceiling. A temporary organ has been placed in this gallery, and a smaller one permanently built in the sanctuary. The high-altar is forty feet high, and the table was constructed in Italy of the purest marble, and inlaid with semi-precious stones. The bas-reliefs on the panels have for their subjects the Divine Passion. The tabernacle over the altar is of white marble, decorated with Roman mosaics and precious stones, and with a door of gilt bronze. The altar of the Blessed Virgin is at the eastern end of the north side-aisle of the sanctuary, and is of carved French walnut. The sacristy is placed in the east of the south aisle of the sanctuary, and St. Joseph's altar, of bronze and mosaic, is in front of it. The altar of the Sacred Heart is of bronze. The four altars cost about one hundred thousand dollars. The Cardinal's throne is on the gospel (right) side of the sanctuary, and is of Gothic design. The altar of the Holy Family is of white Tennessee marble, and the reredos of Caen-stone; over the altar hangs a painting of the Holy Family by Costazzini. There are four hundred and eight pews, of ash, having a seating capacity of twenty-six hundred, and the aisles will afford standing room for nearly as many more. The cathedral is lighted by seventy windows, thirty-seven of which are memorial windows. They were mainly made at Chartres, France, cost about one hundred thousand dollars, and were presented by parishes and individuals in various parts of the country. The total cost of the cathedral, up to the present, has been a trifle over two million

dollars, and it is estimated that at least half a million more will be needed to complete the design. The cathedral was solemnly dedicated, with effective ceremonies, on Sunday, May 25, 1879, by Cardinal McCloskey. Services are held in this church every day.

Church of the Holy Trinity, Madison Avenue, corner of Forty-second Street.

A few words may be said in reference to the church architecture of Fifth Avenue, which is imposing to the spectator from its variety and beauty of form. In one shape or another it has reminiscences of every style. It is Romanesque; it is Byzantine; it is modern flamboyant; it has some characteristics of the positive Renaissance; here and there it suggests the Lombard-Gothic, the Italian, or the Norman; and it is always interesting from its costliness

St. Bartholomew's, Madison Avenue.

and massiveness. One of the specimens of fine church architecture in Fifth Avenue is the Dutch Reformed Church, at the corner of Forty-eighth Street. This is modernized Gothic in style and brown-stone in material; and, if any

fault is to be found with it, it is with the wooden frames to the stained-glass windows, that were put up in the temporizing spirit that spoils so much of the honest architecture of this country.

A striking illustration of the irregular and picturesque style of church-building is the Jewish temple at the corner of Lexington Avenue and Sixty-third Street. The predominant element is the Byzantine, though this is strongly modified by the Gothic, the most pronounced mark of the latter being the great rose-window. The tendency to extreme decoration noticeable in the fanciful trickery of the stone-work in the upper portion of the church is not carried off by the sense of height and mass. But, in spite of this fault, the effect of the church on the eye is highly agreeable—an impression not lessened when the visitor enters the building and takes note of the splendid interior decorations.

The growth of the Jewish element in New York to be such an important factor of life, is very well illustrated in many costly and beautiful synagogues. There are sixteen regular synagogues and temples, and a still larger number of small meeting-houses. Several of the synagogues are specially worthy of notice. That on the corner of Lexington Avenue and Fifty-fifth Street is a fine example of the Greek Byzantine, and its massive proportions and strangely-shaped towers attract the eye with a sense of keen curiosity. This temple is of great size, and was for a long time the most important of the Jewish places of worship in the city of New York.

But a still more noble edifice is the Temple Emanuel, at the northeast corner of Fifth Avenue and Forty-third Street. It is regarded as the noblest specimen of the Saracenic architecture in America, and it is one of the costliest churches in New York. It is built of brown and yellow sandstone, with the roof of alternate lines of red and black tiles. The center of the façade on Fifth Avenue, containing the main entrance, is flanked by two minarets finely carved in open-work. There are five doors leading into the vestibule, from which the interior is reached. Inside the temple the eye is dazzled by a rich profusion of Oriental decoration and coloring.

The Church of the Holy Trinity, at the corner of Madison Avenue and Forty-second Street, is a richly-decorated building in the style of the Renaissance, one striking characteristic being the effect produced by party-colored stones in the walls and the variegated tile-roofing. The edifice is a large one, and the congregation, of which young Dr. Stephen H. Tyng (as he is often called, to distinguish him from his lately deceased father) was for many years the rector, one of the most aristocratic in New York. Two blocks above, on the opposite side of Madison Avenue, the severe lines of St. Bartholomew, marked by its chaste and noble style and its fine Saracenic tower, arrest the attention.

At the corner of Fifty-third Street and Fifth Avenue is St. Thomas's Church, the interior of which is very remarkable in the style of its ornamentation, and specially deserving of a visit; and at the corner of Fifty-fifth Street is the fine church the pastor of which is the famous and eloquent Dr. Hall, who ranks foremost among the Presbyterian divines of the land. The latter church is a simple adaptation of the French Gothic, and the material is of brown-stone. The tower is the loftiest in the city, and the church is regarded as one of the finest specimens of ecclesiastical art, both in its exterior and interior in New York. The power of the preacher attracts great audiences every Sunday.

St. Thomas's Church is also of brown-stone, and its style of architecture is mixed, the Early English predominating. A few words of special description are due to the remarkable interior decoration of this church, executed under the direction of Mr. John La Farge, the artist. With the exception of Trinity Church, Boston, it is the only attempt of the kind yet made in America, worthy to be ranked with interior church decoration as seen in Europe. This unique and beautiful work was prompted by the wish of Mr. Housman, a member of the parish, to commemorate the name of his mother. The form of the choir is seven-sided, five of which are being decorated under Mr. La Farge's design, the sculptured portion of the work being due to Mr. A. St. Gaudens. The general design is a sculptured adoration of the cross by the angels, with paintings on each side representing scenes in the life of Christ immediately following the resurrection.

A description of one of these pictures will give the reader a conception of the whole. The tomb is represented on the left, with the angel sitting on it, and the sleeping guards at the side, while at the right Mary Magdalene throws herself at the feet of the Saviour. It has many features of beauty and picturesqueness, the composition is full of dignity and repose, and the landscape is charming in its suggestion of early dawn. The sculptured portion is fully as interesting. A large cross rises directly above the bishop's chair, and on either side, arranged in four rows, are kneeling angels, who adore the sacred symbol. A large crown is suspended above this cross, and beneath it is a row of cherubic heads. The whole is inclosed between two rich pilasters, designed and in great part executed by Mr. La

Temple Emanuel, corner of Fifth Avenue and Forty-third Street.

Farge himself. The sculptured work is fine in its spirit of joy and cheer, and suggests the early Italian art, though in no sense can it be called a slavish imitation. Mr. St. Gaudens, in his style and method, has returned to the model of the early Italian Renaissance, so inimitable in its commingling of intellectual penetration with deep religious feeling. This is specially seen in the jubilant fullness of expression with which the angels bow and bend before the symbol that unites heaven and earth in healthy happiness, as birds soaring and singing to greet the rising sun. This work in its entirety may be looked on as the pioneer of a new departure in a beautiful school of ecclesiastical art, and it will probably manifest itself more fully in the future. One great difficulty in the way of such decorations comes from the ignorance of church committees as to the nature of the artist's work and the condition under which it is produced. Properly there can be no business relations between the artist and the business-man other than that the artist shall do his work to the best of his ability, and that the business-man shall pay promptly and generously when it is done, and leave him untrammeled while he is doing it.

Let us now cross to the east side of New York, to the old Bowerie farm of Governor Stuyvesant, one of

in his garden, stood until recently at the corner of Thirteenth Street and Third Avenue. On the site of the present St. Mark's Church, Governor Stuyvesant built a chapel at his own expense, and dedicated it to the service of God according to the ritual of the Reformed Dutch Church. At his death he was buried in the vault within the chapel, and over his remains was placed a slab which may still be seen in the eastern wall of St. Mark's, with the following inscription: " In this vault lies buried PETER STUYVESANT, late Captain-General and Commander-in-Chief of Amsterdam, in New Netherlands, now called New York, and the Dutch West India Islands. Died in August, A. D. 1682, aged eighty years." Other tablets and curious monuments of the past are to be found in this quaint old building. When the first building properly known as St. Mark's Church was erected, the locality, which is now in the heart of the older part of the city, was one of

St. Thomas's Church, corner of Fifth Avenue and Fifty-third Street.

the famous rulers of the New Netherlands. Here, the old chronicles tell us, " he enjoyed the repose of agricultural pursuits within the sight of the smoke of the city, which curled above the tree-tops." His house was built of small yellow brick, imported from Holland, and stood near the present St. Mark's Church, on Second Avenue near East Tenth Street. A fine brick building now covers the spot. A pear-tree, imported from Holland by Stuyvesant in 1647, and planted

green fields, and for a long time "St. Mark's in the fields" was the recognized suburban Protestant Episcopal place of worship. St. Mark's is still attended by many old and aristocratic families, for it shares with Trinity and St. Paul's the dignity of age and historical association.

Among the noticeable churches to which attention should be called is St. George's, situated on the corner of East Sixteenth Street and Rutherford Place. This edifice is said to be capable of holding a larger congregation than any other ecclesiastical structure in the city of New York. It is built of solid brown-stone, and, with its two lofty towers looking to the east, and immense depth and height of wall, is certainly entitled to the first rank among the religious edifices of America. It was erected in 1849; but the interior was completely destroyed by fire on the 14th of November, 1865. The refitting of the building was immediately entered upon, and it is now one of the handsomest in the country. The interior is very striking in its polychromatic designs, and the ceiling of the roof is a "thing of beauty" well worth seeing. The chancel is one of the handsomest in the city. The adjoining rectory and the chapel on Sixteenth Street are architecturally and otherwise in keeping with the noble edifice of which they are a part.

Another quaint and charming church is that in Twenty-ninth Street near Fifth Avenue, the Church of the Transfiguration, popularly known as the "Little Church around the Corner," a name bestowed on it by a neighboring clergyman, who, refusing to bury an actor from his own church, referred the applicant to this one. It is rather interesting from its old-fashioned irregularity and air of seclusion, than from any architectural pretensions. Half hidden in a quiet little park of its own, it reminds one of a country church, and this aspect in the heart of a great city strikes the imagination pleasantly. The church is Gothic in the form of a Latin Cross, and contains a number of memorial windows, among them being one dedicated to the memory of the late H. J. Montague the actor. Owing to the incident which gave the church its popular name, almost all members of the theatrical profession, who die in or near New York, are buried from there.

Such are a few of the more striking and characteristic churches of New York, a city peculiarly rich in such edifices, though the sister city of Brooklyn is a rival, for the latter place is well called "The City of Churches."

As has before been remarked, the city is not distinguished by a predominance of pure architectural form in ecclesiastical style. For instance, there are but two or three examples of pure Gothic, and none, so far as we know, of pure Norman. But the somewhat composite character of our church architecture, if it offends the art-purist, is perhaps more pleasing to the general eye; and it is only just to state that the blending of different styles has

Presbyterian Church, Fifth Avenue and Fifty-fifth Street.

St. George's Church, corner of Sixteenth Street and Rutherford Place.

been for the most part accomplished with great good taste and sense of harmony. Most of the fine churches of New York, too, do not offend by that elaborate ornateness of decoration into which the architect is tempted, when he seeks to combine the elements of various styles in his design. Of course, the city can not claim for itself such magnificent creations of the builder's art as may be found in many of the principal European capitals. These were products of an immense religious and art fervor such as is not likely to occur again.

Church of the Transfiguration, Twenty-ninth Street, near Fifth Avenue.

RIVER AND WHARF SCENES.

Scene on the North River.

fleet of grander vessels towers almost over our heads on the rising tide, in their berths. The wealth they contain and the adventures they suggest invest them, as we have said, with no small measure of poetic interest. They are like a glorious army of pilgrims gathered in a central port from the shrines of every nation—gathered with peace-offerings and treasure after trials and victorious conquest.

We see nothing on the New York waterfront like the great wharves and docks which make the maritime accommodations of London and Liverpool so marvelous. The latter, indeed, may almost be included among the wonders of the world, so extensive and commodious are they. It is true, indeed, that the depth of the water does not prescribe such radical and extensive improvements as were made in the two great English cities, but none the less true is it that there has long been felt a need of reconstruction. Various plans have been suggested and experiments made, which

A TOUR around the water-front is full of charm; the scenes and incidents have no common fascination. In its course we can muse away hours, dream ourselves into the tropics or the farthest north, and awaken to a remembrance of the great extent and variety of our seaboard commerce. A myriad of small craft, propelled by steam and sail, flecks the stream. A

6

will be described further on, but they have not so far proved wholly satisfactory.

The architecture of the wharves, and the buildings on them, may be deemed inadequate commercially, but its irregularity, perhaps its very poverty, gives it an artistic value which we should be sorry to miss. The ancient battalions of sail-lofts, ship-chandleries and stores, with swinging sign-boards, have more or less a nautical aspect, and will, no doubt, recall to many some dear old port of their youth. There may be those, indeed, who will regret the time when these weather-beaten structures are swept away, and supplanted by others more commodious, but not more interesting.

Inadequate and unsatisfactory as are the existing wharves, the trade they accommodate will astound the reader who is unversed in commercial statistics. The number of entrances of sailing-vessels engaged in foreign trade for 1880 was 5,775, with a tonnage of 2,917,741 tons; and the number of entrances of steamers the same year was 1,826, with a tonnage of 4,604,652 tons. The number of clearances for the same year (foreign trade) was 5,604 sailing-vessels, with a tonnage of 2,951,349 tons, and 1,833 steamers, with a tonnage of 4,623,265 tons. Referring to the coastwise trade, we find entrances and clearances of 3,376 sailing-vessels, and of 3,018 steamers, with an aggregate of 4,588,654 tons. This shows an aggregate of 21,492 vessels, but, as each vessel is included both in the clearances and entrances, we must estimate one half of the number, or 10,746 vessels, as entering and clearing New York Harbor in the course of the last year. The tonnage of New York fell off very materially during the war, and since that time a large part of the business which was formerly done in American ships has been transferred to foreign bottoms, a drawback from which we have very recently commenced to recover. In spite of this, however, the immense increase in trade and the demand for ocean-carriage has more than counterbalanced the difference, showing a gratifying exhibit in spite of the "hard times," from which commerce has been suffering. When the reader crosses one of the ferries, and views the fringe of shipping, he will have occasion for reflection and wonder, if he bears the above figures in mind.

We may choose any hour for a ramble along the wharves, but the best is in the morning, for then we can see Commerce arouse from its heavy slumbers, and, limb by limb, unfold and apply itself to the great crank that grinds out the nation's destiny. It is, indeed, well worth while to watch the soft shades of morning breaking over Corlear's Hook, and bringing into clearer relief the entangled masts and rigging that are woven against the receding night-clouds; well worth while to watch the gradual change from night to morning, from a desert-like stillness to a fretful roar; to watch the moonbeams driven from their nooks in the silent warehouses, as shutters are thrust aside, doors opened, and living streams pour through every adjacent street to the water-front. The river, smoothly lapping the piers in darkness, breaks into a surfy tumult, as it is beaten and crossed by paddle and oar. Each stone gives forth a rattle, and the inanimate as well as the animate unreins a restless tongue. Gangways are opened to the grand old clippers, and companies of broad-shouldered, labor-marked men trot from deck to wharf, with baskets and barrows. The night-watchmen shuffle homeward to breakfast, with a few others who have been busy during the night, loading and unloading ocean-steamships. Again appear the thick-wheeled drays, drawn by powerful horses, and laden with tons of valuable merchandise. From the masses that throng the river-street, one would think that the whole population of the city had business to do by the water-front, each individual actuated by a different purpose and destiny. The elements contend and bustle; yet we see that they are systematic, and that each man's share of the work helps to give the big wheel a turn.

In making a brief study of the extended water-front of New York and its varied, picturesque associations, let us begin at the Battery, at the extreme southern end of the city, and stroll as fancy dictates, for nowhere can the sight-seer go amiss if he has a quick eye and a little imagination in finding continual food for interesting thought.

As one looks down the shining bay from the Battery, the scene is one which impresses itself on the imagination beyond the possibility of forgetting. The crowded shipping going and coming, steamers being slowly drawn by puffing tugs, stately ships preparing for their long voyages, fishing and oyster boats, yachts, men-of-war, small sail-boats, etc., make up a scene animated in the extreme. The bright waters shining with sunbeams seem to be fairly alive, as they dance along the surface of the bay; and the islands in the harbor, with their glimpses of greenery lifting above the swift tides, add to the variety and attraction of the outlook. The imagination conjures up visions of these outgoing and incoming vessels, which bind New York with all parts of the world, floating over tropical

View of the Bay from the Battery.

seas, or battling with the savage fury of wind and wave thousands of miles away, until the prosaic and bustling present sinks out of sight, and one realizes the infinite labor, suffering, and patience, the tax laid on human bravery, endurance, and skill, to carry on the intricate relations of commerce. The Battery is always fringed with sight-seers and loungers, who appear to gaze on the brilliant scene with constant delight; for nowhere in New York is there more to fill the eye and stimulate the fancy.

At the Battery is Castle Garden, now used as an immigrant depot, where those who come from the Old to seek homes in the New World first find a resting-place, and receive their earliest impression of their new country. Castle Garden is an historic spot, having been originally a fort and afterward a summer garden, whence it derives its now not very appropriate name. It was once used for civic and military displays and receptions, and it was here that Lafayette received the honor of a grand ball in 1824, when he revisited the country to which he had so gallantly given his military services. Other celebrated men also received public receptions on this historic spot. It was here also that Jenny Lind made her first appearance under P. T. Barnum's management, and sang before the most

Landing-Steps, west of the Battery.

brilliant and numerous audiences which ever applauded the notes of a singer in America.

By-and-by, as the town grew far away from this region, Castle Garden was given up as a place of resort, and converted in 1855 to the use of immigrants by the erection of suitable accommodations. The European steamers, which bring these tides of living freight, land them at this spot, where they receive food and shelter till such time as they are ready to start for their destinations. There was a time when the Garden was infested with immigrant-runners, who preyed on the ignorant and timid strangers, for the most part unable to speak any English, without mercy. But this has now been suppressed, and the poor foreigner is fed, protected, sheltered, and transported with his worldly goods to the station, when he departs for the land of milk and honey which he hopes to find. At times there are not less than a thousand immigrants sheltered here, and it is a most interesting and suggestive spectacle.

Here one may see all manner of strange garbs from all parts of Europe, and hear a babel of polyglot sounds, as the newly-arrived aspirants for American citizenship with their wives and babies, spend a few brief days, preparing for departure. A fortnight hence they will have been scattered from Minnesota to Texas, from Maine to the Golden Gate of the Pacific, and fairly em-

North River Flotilla

barked on the life which is to assimilate them with the wonderful facts and forces of the great republic of the West.

The system of caring for the immigrants is simple, but thorough and satisfactory. After examination of their luggage on shipboard by the customs officers, the immigrants are transferred to this landing depot, where they are received by officers of the Commission, who enter in registers kept for the purpose all necessary particulars for their future identification. The names of such as have money, letters, or friends awaiting them, are called out, and they are put into immediate possession of their property, or committed to their friends, whose credentials have first been properly scrutinized. Such as desire can find clerks at hand to write letters for them in any European language, and a telegraph operator within the depot to forward dispatches. Here, also, the main trunk lines of railway have offices, at which the immigrant can buy tickets and have his luggage weighed and checked; brokers are admitted (under restrictions which make fraud impossible) to exchange the foreign coin or paper of immigrants; a restaurant supplies them with plain food at moderate prices; a physician is in attendance for the sick; a temporary hospital is ready to receive them until they can be conveyed to Ward's Island; and those in search of employment are furnished it at the labor bureau connected with the establishment. Such as desire to start at once are sent to the railway or steamboat, while those who prefer to remain in the city are referred to boarding-house keepers whose charges are regulated by, and houses kept under the supervision of, the Commissioners. The old scandals and abuses have long since disappeared under the new method.

If picturesqueness were the only thing de-

Ferry Boat at Night.

sirable in the water-front of a great seaport, that of New York would be everything needful, but the picturesque is oftentimes opposed to the convenient; and, as one looks on the dilapidated old piers, narrow streets, and tumble-down rookeries of warehouses, their insufficiency becomes plain. For many years the commercial interests of the city have suffered from bad wharfage,

but there has been a beginning of better things, and suitable piers are now in process of erection.

The total available water frontage of New York, not counting the New Jersey and Long Island shores, which are equally devoted to the accommodation of the shipping interest of the city, is twenty-four and three fourths miles.

"It is evident," General McClellan wrote when

An Ocean-Steamer in Dock.

Engineer of the Dock Department, "that we need not resort to the English system of inclosed docks. The arrangement best suited to our wants is a continuous river-wall, so located as to widen the river-street very considerably, with ample covered piers projecting from it. This is the simplest, most convenient, and by far the most economical system that can be suggested. It will bring into play all the extraordinary natural advantages of the port, and will give every facility for the

cheap and rapid handling of vessels and their cargoes." The plans proposed by General McClellan, approved by the Dock Commissioners, and now being carried out with certain modifications, are as follows: 1. A permanent river-wall of *béton* and masonry, or masonry alone, so far outside the existing wharf-line as to give a river-street two hundred and fifty feet wide along the North River, two hundred feet wide along the East River, from the southern extremity of the city to Thirty-first Street, and one hundred and seventy-five feet wide along both streets above that point. 2. A series of piers projecting from the river-wall, of ample dimensions and adequate construction, which will allow an unobstructed passage of the water. 3. The erection of sheds over these piers suitable to the requirements of the vessels using them. The same distinguished engineer says: "I have no doubt as to the immediate necessity of widening the river-streets and building a permanent river-wall; but I think it sound policy to content ourselves with piers of a cheap material, leaving for other generations richer than ours the construction of more permanent structures." It is a fascinating thought for the lover of New York and its greatness to look forward to the time when crazy old jetties and sheds and worm-eaten wooden docks shall be demolished; when firm granite or concrete piers, extending from a broad river-street belting the city in its embrace, shall give complete accommodation to the shipping and commerce of the world; when capacious and well-built warehouses fronting these splendid

An Ocean-Steamer outward bound.

docks shall receive the products of every clime, but this fruition it is to be feared is not to be looked for in our generation, unless some change is made in the system under which our city affairs are administered.

Both day and night the New York waters present a most animated and pleasing sight. It is a characteristic and frequent thing to see in the North River a long line of canal boats towed by tug or steamer on their way from the Erie Canal. These flotillas give a curious character to the appearance of the river, and play a very important part in the commerce of the port. One may also see a little fleet of barges towed by a lumbering and dilapidated steamer, which has survived its gala-days, when gayly decorated with bunting it pursued its stately track up and down the river laden with passengers. The vessels which vary the aspect of the North River front are highly miscellaneous in their composition. Survivals of those ancient crafts which, a hundred years ago, did most of the internal and coastwise commerce of the port, sloops and schooners of antiquated cut, may still be seen crawling over the waters. These Rip Van Winkle vessels which lazily serve the local needs of many of the Hudson River and New Jersey towns and villages, with their battered hulls and patched sails, to the

North River Oyster-Boats.

artist eye are more picturesque than even the trim clipper, with her beautiful lines and tapering spars. They are the links between the past and the present, and their old-fashioned aspect carries one back to the times when steam was unknown, and the age was leisurely, easy-going, simple-minded, and easily contented.

As we have said, the vessels which lie in the harbor are of all kinds and descriptions. Among these may be seen often, specially in the late spring, just before the cruising season begins, many beautiful yachts. The yacht among boats may be likened to the fashionable fine lady, polished, dainty, symmetrical, with an air of grace and distinction not to be mistaken. This airy creation of the ship-builder's adze and hammer carries with it the most delightful association of sea and air, the union of the highest luxury of civilization with the primitive delight in the rich heritage of the blue sky, exhilarating breezes, and the glancing waters. Yachting as carried on in New York costs a great deal of money, and it is as much the favorite amusement of the wealthy as the ownership of fine horses. Twelve yacht-clubs have their headquarters in or near New York, the most important being known as the New York Club, which has a total tonnage of about five thousand tons, and an estimated valuation of vessels amounting to three million dollars.

Gliding in and out among these beautifully shaped crafts, with their graceful lines and taper-ing spars, may be seen the sturdy and democratic little tugs, full of compact grit and energy, which puff along, towing, perhaps, several vessels twenty times their size, with an air of ease which astonishes one's mind, and conveys a sense of compressed power not surpassed by one's notion of a British bull-dog or a can of nitro-glycerine, though in this case it is force conservative and useful, not destructive. The waters of such a great harbor are full of surprises and contrasts of form and function, and the philosopher finds no end of food for his humor and fancy as well as his edification in the survey thereof. We behold the river-surface plowed by every kind of vessel. Squat ferry-boats, like enormous turtles, black with passengers; splendid steamboats, with tier on tier of staterooms; capacious barges; row-boats, dancing along like cockle-shells; solid and queer-looking dredging-machines and pile-drivers; dingy sloops and schooners—all dodge each other in this moving pageant of the broad stream, which is more like an arm of the sea than an ordinary river, in its suggestion to the mind.

When the shadows of night settle down over the waters of New York, the scene is no less picturesque. Lights flash far and wide over the faintly-gleaming surface of river and bay, and hoarse, far-distant cries echo along the wharves and from ship to ship, showing the presence of life, quiescent, but not entirely asleep. From time to time the white sails of ships glide by like giant specters, while on the opposite shores gleam the street-lamps of sister cities like an army of fire-flies. When a heavy fog settles on the river, wiping out as with a sponge the distant lights, there is something weird and oppressive in the scene. Darkness shrouds the outlook, but through the thick, black air the shrill shrieking of the steam-whistles keeps up an incessent cacophony. Suddenly there shoots out of the gloom a great eyeball of light, which is speedily multiplied into many as the ferry-boat nears the landing. So great are the skill and care of the pilots of the ferry-boats, that collisions rarely occur even on the most foggy nights, which, in view of the great number and constant running of these transit-boats, is a matter of marvel.

It is along the wharves at night, particularly on very dark and foggy nights, that the river-thieves find their sphere of operations. The riches lying along the wharves tempt theft, and organized bands of these criminals ply a lucrative business in miscellaneous stealing of everything not under the closest watch. They often, too, indulge in broad acts of piracy, boarding vessels, gagging the crew, and not unseldom committing murder. Some of their outrages are of the most audacious character, for these bands contain many of the most reckless and daring scoundrels hatched out of the rotten compost of our civilization. A special corps of river-police patrols the waters in a small steamer on the outlook for these daring ruffians, and watching with suspicious eyes all the small craft and row-boats that ply along the shores, for what to untrained eyes would be a mere pleasure-boat, might contain a crew of these bold pirates. The strongholds of these thieves shift from time to time to elude the watchful guardians of the public peace and property, now being in some hut on a quiet sand-beach down the bay, now under one of the unfrequented piers far up town. A spot which has been specially noted in police annals for the operations of these rascals, than whom there are none more bold and cunning in New York, is Corlear's Hook, which is at the bend of the East River, just below Grand Street, and opposite the Brooklyn Navy-Yard. Large machine-shops and storage warehouses make this part of the New York water-front almost deserted at night, and afford the thieves ample chance to sally out and return with their booty unobserved, while squalid rookeries and tenements near at hand furnish places of convenient concealment.

Perhaps there is no part of the water-front of the city more attractive than those quays and streets on the North River where we almost pass under the bowsprits of the immense ocean-steam-ships of the Pacific Mail Company, the Inman line, the White Star line, the State line, and others which bring us thousands of tourists and immigrants, and the most valuable freights. The

The Canal-Boats, East River.

arrival or departure of one of these fine triumphs of marine architecture is a picturesque and animating sight. The great ship itself, viewed as a study of man's scientific mastery in his combat with Nature, is a marvel in completeness of make and equipment, alike to defy the treacherous moods of the sea, and to subserve all the comforts and luxuries of man.

European steamers leave and arrive at the port of New York daily, sometimes half a dozen in a single day, and, in addition to these great ships that ply over the ocean-ferry to Europe, there are lines to South and Central America, the West Indies, the Windward Islands, to Florida, New Orleans, Texas, Mexico, Cuba, and various other domestic and foreign destinations. Among the European lines the Cunard has long been famous for its immunity from accident. The White Star line is widely known for its large, admirably equipped, and swift vessels; and the Williams & Guion line has at the head of its fleet the largest steamship in the world, the Arizona, with the exception of the Great Eastern. An ocean-steamer is a vast floating hotel, where

Wharf-Scene.

rich and poor find accommodations to suit their means and their tastes. When one of these great vessels, decked with flags, and crowded with people on its decks, waving handkerchiefs to their friends ashore, moves out of the wharf, it is one of the most striking and suggestive scenes to be witnessed on the water-front of the city, fruitful as it is in interesting suggestions. Although the stormy Atlantic has become merely a great ocean-ferry, an occasional terrible disaster by storm or fire still invests travel across its long leagues of sea with that dim suggestion of tragedy and horror which always belongs to the unknown. The scenes consequent on the arrival of an ocean-steamer have also their interesting phases, often mixed with a dash of the ludicrous, which grow out of the inspection of baggage by the Custom-House officers.

For those visitors to New York, who may be contemplating foreign travel, it may be useful and interesting, in this connection, to learn something of the *modus operandi* of the Custom-House officials on the arrival of any steamship from a foreign port. The baggage of passengers is landed on the steamship-wharf as soon as practical after the vessel is docked. But, before any baggage

Fish-Market, East River.

is delivered, each passenger is required to make, under oath, an entry of his or her baggage, and a separate entry, also under oath, of all articles contained in his or her baggage which, by the United States laws, are subject to duty, and to pay such duty, if any. The blank forms of the entries to be made are (if practicable) furnished to each passenger after the vessel leaves quarantine by the customs officers, who also give the passenger all necessary information relative thereto.

Fishing-Boats in Dock.

In case no customs officers come on board at quarantine, the forms of entries are furnished when the vessel arrives at her wharf. The senior member of a family coming together, if sufficiently acquainted with the contents of the baggage of the whole party to make a sworn statement of the same, is allowed to include all such baggage in one entry. Whenever any trunk or package brought by a passenger as baggage contains articles subject to duty, and the value thereof exceeds five hundred dollars, or if the quantity or variety of the dutiable articles is such that a proper examination, classification, or appraisement can not be made at the vessel, the trunk or package is sent to the public store for appraisement. Passengers will find it useful to remember that wearing-apparel to be free must not only have been worn, but must show signs of wear; the intention to wear it one's self is not sufficient. Jewelry that has been worn or is in use as a personal ornament is admitted free, but duty is demanded on all watches but one brought in by a single passenger, even if all of them are old. In spite of the vigilance of the revenue officials, who watch with lynx-eyes every attempt to infringe on the regulations, there are not a few successful smugglers. Fair ladies, who belong to the most aristocratic circles, do not at times think it either sinful or undignified to evade paying duty on costly laces, gloves, jewelry, and similar articles of luxury. The moral casuistry, by which one is persuaded that cheating the Government out of such small matters as customs dues is rather creditable than otherwise, is of the simplest kind, and almost intuitively appreciated by most people except the Government officials. The fun for the bystander is when one of these gentry detects the offense. The ruthless severity with which trunks and other baggage are then examined and tossed about piece by piece, the dismay of the fair offender and her friends, and the excitement and curiosity of the wharf-loungers and workmen, make quite a little comedy. These occurrences occasionally appear in print; but, if the stories of the customs officials be true, most of the facts are quietly hushed up and kept from the knowledge of the eager and active reporter.

The wharves are generally crowded with stevedores and other laborers busy in loading and unloading ships, and a continual succession of drays is going and coming, making the approaches more than ordinarily difficult to the foot passenger, who hears, in an hour, if he is not familiar with the *argot* of blasphemy, more sulphurous language in this quarter than he would otherwise

learn in a month. The business of the stevedore is one requiring special skill and knowledge, as the problem of packing away the multifarious freight in the most compact form without too much interfering with the balance of the ship is not an easy one to solve. In and out of the swarm of laborers darts the ragged gutter-snipe, his sharp eye cocked for a chance to steal any article, if it be only an orange or a cocoanut, whenever the attention of the policeman is turned away from him. Accidents are not uncommon along the water-front, and one wonders that they are not more frequent. Strong men with bare breasts and arms, sweating in the hot sun, toil up and down the narrow gang-plank from ship to shore in an endless file, bearing on their stooping shoulders great burdens of barrels, boxes, bales, etc. Suddenly one of these human dray-horses slips and falls a dozen feet or more, crushed and mangled. Such is a passing episode, quickly accomplished and soon forgotten in the tumult of human interests surging around; but it means untold misery and wretchedness to a few hearts.

A brief walk from the great wharves of the North River carries us fairly into the heart of the produce trade which monopolizes West Street, from Canal Street to the Battery, and most of the intersecting streets as far back as Greenwich Street. Flour, meal, butter, eggs, cheese, meats, poultry, fish, cram the tall warehouses and rude sheds, teeming at the water's edge to their fullest capacity. Fruit-famed New Jersey pours four fifths of its produce into this lap of distributive commerce; the river-hugging counties above contribute their share; and carloads come trundling in from the West to feed the perpetually hungry maw of the Empire City.

The concentration of this great and stirring trade is to be met with at Washington Market. This vast wooden structure, with its numerous outbuildings and sheds, is an irregular and unsightly one, but presents a most novel and interesting scene within and without. The sheds are mainly devoted to smaller stands and smaller sales. Women with baskets of fish and tubs of tripe on their heads, lusty butcher-boys lugging halves or quarters of beef or mutton into their carts, peddlers of every description, etc., tend to amuse and bewilder at the same time. Some of the produce dealers and brokers, who occupy the little box-like shanties facing the market from the river, do a business almost as large as any of the neighboring merchants boasting their five-story warehouses. The sidewalks some years ago were so clogged up by booths that passage was seriously impeded; but this nuisance has

East River Bridge, between New York and Brooklyn.

Dry-Dock.

been somewhat abated, though there is still a great chance for improvement.

An interesting feature of the North River front will be found in the great wholesale oyster-boats, consisting of rusty and dilapidated-looking barges, moored by the stern to the wharves. Into these receptacles the sloops engaged in the oyster-trade discharge their cargoes, and thence the luscious bivalve is distributed to dealers in all parts of the city. Oysters are brought to New York from points as far south as Virginia and Maryland, and from the northern coast as far as Boston, but the bulk of them come from the inlets of the New Jersey coast and Long Island Sound. So valuable has the oyster business become, that acres of salt-water within fifty miles of New York, in favorable localities, are worth several fold the same area of dry land. Some oyster-farmers send to the city from one hundred to two hundred thousand bushels every season, and not a few become wealthy in a few years in pursuing this business. The seed-oysters are brought from the South, and are said to acquire their peculiar flavor by planting in Northern waters, though the epicures of Baltimore, Washington, and Richmond contemptuously deny this allegation of superior excellence. Oysters are good and plentiful in New York at all seasons of the year, in spite of the popular notion that they are only fit for food from September to May. The trade, however, during the summer months is not active, and the oyster-merchants in their floating warehouses on the North River look disconsolate till the months containing the magical R pass by and bring in the stirring season again.

At the southern end of the East River waterfront we find the canal-boats which receive the freight of the Erie Canal, and the locality is so deceptive in its quietness that a stranger would never suspect the immense commerce which belongs to it. The turtle-like crafts, painted generally in the most grotesquely glaring colors, are so closely moored together, that one can easily walk across them from wharf to wharf. Men, women, and mayhap children, may be seen from time to time on their decks, and strings of family washing flutter in the breeze like ships' bunting. One may see a cradle here, a dog there, and, perhaps, glaring at him from the next old tub, a belligerent tomcat. Here and there we may also see lace curtains at the windows, and flowers peeping from behind—in a word, all the signs of pleasant domesticity. If, like Asmodeus, we could see through the decks, we should probably find the stern divided into three or four compartments, provided with all the comforts for a small family, even to parlor-organs and sewing-machines. The canal-boatmen have their homes on board these vessels, and oftentimes show no little taste in fitting them up. There was a time, many years ago, when these canal-men were a rough and quarrelsome lot, and many were the furious fights, oftentimes ending in homicide, which occurred. Like the flat-boatmen of the West, they were passionate, truculent, and revengeful, though with many good qualities. But things have changed with this class of late years, and they are now as commonplace and orderly as any exposed by the nature of things to a laborious and severe life.

The principal lines of transportation from the West to the East include about ten thousand miles of railway, seven thousand miles of river,

sixteen hundred miles of lake, and sixteen hundred miles of canal. The total freight carried over them in one year is about ten million tons, one fourth of which is transported by boats through the Erie Canal and down the Hudson River, a striking exhibit, which is emphasized by the fact that the canal is only open for six months in the year. The boats travel over ten million miles a season, and give employment to about twenty-eight thousand men and sixteen thousand horses and mules. Passing through the quiet valleys of the Genesee and the Mohawk, they appear so primitive in structure and slow in motion that few persons unfamiliar with the facts would be willing to give them credit for much usefulness; they are towed on the river in long strings by great, white tow-boats, but, inert as they apparently are, their services to commerce far surpass those of the railway, whose trains travel in one day a greater distance than the boats travel in a week.

Wall Street Ferry passed, with its crowds of passengers and vehicles, we glance at a dock full of the fruit-schooners that bring to the city oranges, bananas, lemons, and grapes, from the tropics. No city in the world out of the tropics can show such a variety of luscious fruits. The immense contrast of climate within our own bor-

Navy-Yard, Brooklyn.

ders, and the proximity of New York to the West Indies, the most luxuriant fruit-producing region of the world, fills the market in turn with the most delicious products of vegetable nature. The sight of the booths in the fruit-market, with its burden of rich and varied color, is a study for the painter in its rich luxuriance of hues, as well as suggestive to the epicure.

As the sight-seer strolls from wharf to wharf, he constantly sees something new to strike his attention. Here is the little Florida orange-schooner, with her sun-stained and shaggy sails and cordage, and boatmen still more brown and shaggy. There is a Cuban brigantine, with its richly odorous pineapples and bananas, and we can almost smell the balmy tropical breezes and

see the glowing splendor of tropical vegetation as we give fancy the rein, and find ourselves transported thousands of miles away. We behold on the wharves cargoes of aromatic teas from China and Japan, pungent hides from Texas and Buenos Ayres, huge swollen bales of white cotton from Louisiana, coffees from Brazil and Venezuela, expensive silks and wines from France. The commerce of the most widely scattered zones is emptied on these shabby wharves in kingly profusion, and, among it all, lounges some swart and bearded sailor, whose gay bandana and silver ear-rings show a being distinct from any ordinary type in his life, his tastes, and his notions.

But here we find a fleet of smacks moored,

A Misty Morning.

which sends thought in a different direction, and recalls to fancy the stiff breezes and shining billows that toss the fisher-craft off the Newfoundland Banks. We are at the Fulton Ferry Fish-Market. This stands on the river-side of South Street, north of the ferry-house, and is a long, low frame building of neat appearance, which is maintained by private enterprise. The fishing schooners and sloops discharge their cargoes at the market from the adjacent slips, and the fish are then laid out in attractive fashion on marble slabs or stored in bulk in great ice-chests. In the early morning the place is made a bedlam by the throngs of licensed venders and up-town retail dealers, laying in and carting away their daily supplies.

As we stand here, by the Fulton Ferry dock,

the Great East River Bridge looms up in its grand proportions, and we stop to admire one of the finest specimens of bridge-engineering in the world. We can not do better than give our readers some brief description of this lofty roadway, across which so much of the travel and traffic between the two cities will ere long pass.

The number of people who annually cross the river is now probably but little short of eighty million. The inadequacy of the ferries to accommodate the immense number of persons daily crossing between the two cities, and the interruptions so often caused by fog and ice, led to the project of constructing this great bridge, which is not likely to be fully completed for another year, at least. The Brooklyn terminus will be in the square bounded by Fulton, Prospeet, Sands, and Washington Streets; the New York terminus in Chatham Square, opposite the City Hall Park. The supporting tower on the New York side is at Pier No. 29, near the foot of Roosevelt Street; and the corresponding tower in Brooklyn is just north of the Fulton Ferry-house.

The bridge may be divided into five parts: the central span across the river from tower to tower, fifteen hundred and ninety-five feet long; a span on each side from the tower to the anchorage, nine hundred and forty feet long; and the approaches from the terminus to the anchorage on each side. The total length of the bridge closely approaches six thousand feet. The width, of eighty-five feet, will include a promenade of thirteen feet, two railroad-tracks, and four wagon or horse-car tracks. From high-water mark to the floor of the bridge in the center will be a distance of one hundred and thirty-five feet, a height considered great enough to remove all impediment to free navigation. The central span is suspended from four cables of steel wire, each sixteen inches in diameter, which are assisted by stays, the cables having a deflection of one hundred and twenty-eight feet. Each tower rests immediately on a caisson,

below the upper cornice at the top these dimensions are reduced, by sloped offsets at intervals, to one hundred and twenty feet by forty. The total height above high water of each tower

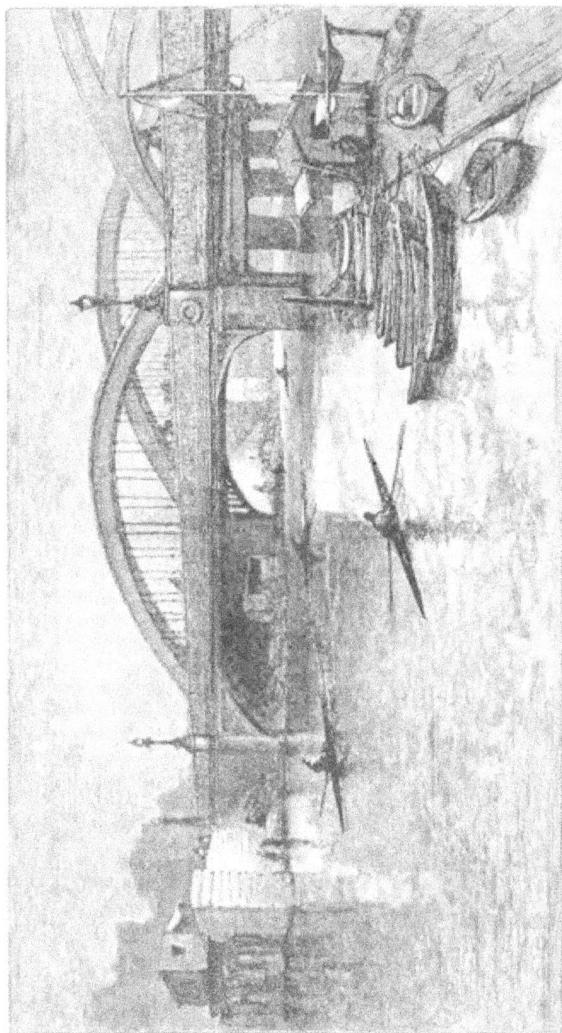

Harlem Bridge

is two hundred and sixty-eight feet. At the anchorages each of the four cables, after passing over the towers, enters the anchor-walls at an elevation of nearly eighty feet above high water, and passes through the masonry a distance

sunk to the rock beneath the river, this being on the New York side about ninety feet below the surface of the water. The towers erected upon these foundations are one hundred and thirty-four by fifty-six feet at the water-line;

7

Harlem River on a Holiday.

of twenty feet, at which point a connection is formed with the anchor-chains. Each anchorage contains about thirty-five thousand cubic yards of masonry. The spans from the anchorages to the towers are suspended to the cables, and carried over the roofs of the buildings underneath. The approach on the Brooklyn side from the terminus to the anchorage measures eight hundred and thirty-six feet; on the New York side, thirteen hundred and thirty-six feet. These approaches are supported by iron girders and trusses, which will rest at short intervals upon piers of masonry, or iron columns built within the blocks crossed and occupied. The streets are crossed by stone arches at such elevations as to leave them unobstructed. The Brooklyn terminus is sixty-eight feet above high tide. The cost has already largely exceeded the original estimate for the entire work, and before it is fully completed some fifteen million dollars will in all probability have been expended. The heavy masonry for the anchorages and street approaches is at the time of this writing far advanced toward completion in both New York and Brooklyn.

It has been proposed to have both steam and horse-car transit over the bridge, and, if this is accomplished, it will be not only an important result in railroad economy as applied to city travel, but a most picturesque and striking fact in our city life. In all essential ways New York and Brooklyn must be regarded as the one metropolis, and nowhere else in the world will the eye be greeted with lines of metropolitan traffic and travel running one hundred and thirty-five feet above the water-level.

Hurrying past Roosevelt, Hunter's Point, and Catharine Street Ferries, we are next curiously struck in contemplating the system of dry docks. Marvelously crazy, rotten, twisted, unsightly objects these dry docks are, but they are most important adjuncts to the marine interests of New York, for it is here that vessels are put in hospital

High Bridge.

for repairs. We draw near the iron-foundries and the gas-works as we pass along in our tour of inspection, and the shipping begins to be less thick, the traffic less noisy. A common sight in this neighborhood is a battered old turret-ship or an old frigate lying in ordinary at moorings. Not only have there been built here the huge boilers and ponderous engines of many an ocean-steamer, but the iron sides of the steamers themselves have been fused, and cast, and shaped, and bolted, and built on this spot. You note your approach to the works by the overflow of superfluous iron-ware. Vast, rusty, propped-up caverns of iron confront you; abandoned boilers, big enough for church-steeples, encumber all the highways; smaller fragments of iron, of manifold mysterious shapes, lie piled up on every curbstone. Then appear the tall walls, the great chimneys, and all the horrible confusion of vast work-yards and workshops. All about is grimy

and repulsive. The mud is black with coal-dust; the pools of water dark and dismal; the low, rotten, wretched houses clustering about, damp and sooty; all the faces, and all the walls, and all the posts, and every object, grimy and soiled; while the distracting din of innumerable hammers "closing rivets up" unites in rendering the whole scene purgatorial. A great industry and source of wealth is the iron interest, but the manipulation of that indispensable metal has abundant harsh and discordant features. Beyond the iron-works are more ship-yards, more ferries, more vessels, with wharf-building, lot-filling, dirt-dumping, and what-not.

A brief glance at the Brooklyn Navy-Yard, which is on the south shore of Wallabout Bay, and about opposite Corlear's Hook, will be of interest to the reader. This is the principal naval station in the country, and the grounds embrace a total area of one hundred and forty-four acres, including more than a mile of splendid wharfage. About two thousand men are employed here almost constantly, and the station is under the command of a commodore of the United States Navy. The visitor will find here a myriad of things to interest his attention, but over these we must pass hastily with a brief description of the immense dry dock, which is one of the most remarkable structures of the kind in the world. It is built of granite, and the main chamber is two hundred and eighty-six feet long by thirty-five feet wide at the bottom, and three hundred and seven feet long by ninety-eight feet wide at the top, with a depth of thirty-six feet. The enormous steam-pumps connected with the dock can empty it of water in four and a half hours. This dock cost considerably over two million dollars.

The United States Naval Lyceum, founded by officers of the Navy in 1833, is situated in the Navy-Yard. It has a fine library and a large collection of curiosities, together with valuable geological and mineralogical cabinets. Just east of the Navy-Yard are extensive marine barracks, and on the opposite side of Wallabout Bay is the Marine Hospital, a handsome structure surrounded by twenty-one acres of ground, and having accommodations for five hundred patients. The yard is under the command of a commodore of the United States Navy.

Crossing to the New York side again and hastening up the line of wharves, at last we reach the upper portion of the East River waterfront, where we seem to have passed out of the domain of commerce and manufacture, and a kind of lazy life pervades the docks almost as sluggish and easy-going as that of some roasting port. Ferry-boats and steamboats plow the river, and a fleet of sail and row boats glide pleasantly over the calm water, suggestive of anything but the bustle and turmoil of a great city. As we approach Harlem Bridge, which crosses the Harlem River at One Hundred and Twenty-ninth Street and Third Avenue, the scene is picturesque and attractive.

In this vicinity a large number of boat-clubs have their headquarters, and here most of the races occur. On any pleasant day, as one stands on the bridge, he will see racing-shells flash through the water propelled by brawny arms. Boats are always found here to let, either for pleasure-parties or exercise with the single scull, and it need not be said that Harlem Bridge is a favorite resort for the young athletes of the city.

On a holiday the river presents a most gay and lively aspect. Steamboats, steam-launches, and small crafts, loaded with pleasure-seekers, fill the water on all sides, and row-boats glide in and out under the swift strokes of athletic oarsmen. Everybody seems bent on pleasure, but amid the joyous crowd we see little confusion and hear no loud oaths, for it is the more orderly and decent class that seeks diversion in this quarter. Perhaps nowhere in New York or its environs can be witnessed a more breezy, picturesque, and exhilarating scene than the Harlem River on one of these occasions, when everybody is bent for an outing on the water.

Farther up the Harlem River, at One Hundred and Seventy-fifth Street, we reach High Bridge, on which the Croton Aqueduct is carried across the river and valley. The bridge is fourteen hundred and sixty feet long, and supported by thirteen arches resting on solid granite piers, the crown of the highest arch being one hundred and sixteen feet above the water-level. The water is carried over the bridge in large cast-iron pipes protected by brick masonry. The visitor, as he strolls over the fine footpath on the bridge, has a noble prospect greeting his eyes, well repaying him for the trouble of his journey. There are several hotels and restaurants in the vicinity, and this locality has for a long while been a favorite one for Sunday and holiday excursions. On the left or island side of the river are a handsome high-service tower and engine-house, which play an important part in raising the distributing source to the proper level for service in supplying Croton water to the upper part of the city. With the new facilities of transit recently furnished by the completion of the railroad-bridge, enabling the cars of the Metropolitan Elevated road to reach High Bridge, there is no reason why this should not become one of the favorite resorts of the holiday seekers of New York. The air is deliciously pure and cool even on warm days, the landscape a most charming one, and there are a variety of pleasant rural strolls on both sides of the river, with easy passage from one to the other.

In our rapid glance at the extended waterfront of New York, it goes without saying that many interesting facts have been passed unnoticed, but enough has been said to show the visitor to the Empire City what a fund for suggestive thought as well as amusement is offered to him in making a circuit of the wharves which fringe the borders of New York.

ARCHITECTURAL FEATURES.

NOWHERE in the world have so many different styles of building found expression as in the United States. The fact that there is no special style which is the outcome of our people and our national life, none indigenous to our soil, united with the alert and eclectic mind of the American, has resulted in great multiplicity of architectural motive and ornament. Not only is this the case, but it is no less true that many of our most pleasing structures are composite in their character, presenting features of different styles, which are often blended into artistic unity

Roof and Windows, corner Fifth Avenue and Fifty-seventh Street.

with much ingenuity and knowledge, though it is not uncommon again to observe occasional incongruity in these ambitious attempts.

The student of New York buildings will discover specimens of every kind, from battlemented and turreted imitations of the castles of the middle ages to the high-roofed French houses which contain one or two stories above the cornice. In these latter the retreating slant of the roof, as well as the slightly receding sidewall of the house itself, has served to give the occupants more light and air than would be afforded in the winter time by straight façades in the narrow and dark streets of old Paris. Many of the buildings are picturesque and agreeable to the eye, and for their pleasant qualities of form we are glad to see them springing up in the midst of our own cities, whose climatic or political necessities are totally different from those that gave them birth. We conceive that pleasant things or beautiful things, within certain limits, are their own reason for being, if these qualities do not interfere with more serious uses, a consideration always important.

A style in considerable vogue is that of the French château, with its turrets of different shapes, finials, quaintly decorated chimneys, etc., giving an impression of great airiness and lightness, no matter how massive and solid the general structure. In the magnificent Vanderbilt house, on the corner of Fifth Avenue and Fifty-seventh Street, this French château style is considerably modified by old Dutch characteristics, these features being carried out with great elaboration and variety in the ornamentation. It may be a question whether this profusion of decoration produces on the whole as pleasant an effect on the eye as would a greater unity and simplicity, but assuredly the most carping critic could not go so far as to call it meretricious, as in the general effect we discern some relation of ornament to use. This is particularly noticeable in the modified Dutch windows, which in connection with the chimneys break the sky-line so picturesquely, and suggest light, air, and cheerfulness in the interior. In some particulars this house resembles that of another member of the Vanderbilt family, at the corner of Fifty-second street and the same avenue (see p. 30). Both houses are striking and unique in design, and are notable examples of recent outcomes of architectural art.

Nowhere in New York can be seen a greater variety of architectural features in private houses than in Fifty-seventh Street, where for half a dozen squares the eye is continually delighted with striking and original forms. This is alike noticeable in the porches, the windows, and the general effect of the front. We observe in these novel structures a pleasing irregularity, which is independent of old conventional notions, and a daring of design, which has been carried out with enough harmony of detail to relieve it from the imputation of the grotesque, while it fascinates the fancy by its freshness and piquancy.

Between Fifth and Sixth Avenues in Fifty-seventh Street may be seen a group of houses which illustrate this admirably. There is such a quaint confusion in the façades of these houses as to make them difficult to describe. The first one on the left of the illustration is peculiarly novel in style. The low, flat steps leading from the street at an angle, give an air of seclusion and privacy to the porch without detracting from its openness. This peculiarity of the porch, as we shall see more fully further on, is a feature of many of the newer New York houses. The two bay-windows of the house which we are now noticing make the most curious characteristic of its front. The outer projections of the lower window sweep upward in a long curve, making an apparent foundation for the upper window, which extends farther outward, the two windows thus offering an appearance of unity of design and structure. The imagination sees, behind this decorative effect given the front, a fullness and airiness of outlook from the interior, which come of this arrangement, that make the house very charming. For, even to the observer of the exterior of a house, where human beings make their home, there is a disposition to judge the char-

Façades, Fifty-seventh Street, between Fifth and Sixth Avenues.

acter of the front and the general external appearance with some reference to a guess at its adaptability for the uses of those that dwell therein. In the adjoining house represented in the illustration, the approach is even more indirect, there being two angles in the line of steps. The deep porch, the massive bay-window of the first story, the heavy window-copings and lintels, and the broad and rich but simple decoration of the façade combine to present a pleasant picture, full of home-like suggestions. In both of these residences there is great individuality of taste, alike in the general lines and the treatment of ornament.

In Madison Avenue, near Fortieth Street, the eye is attracted by a row of fine residences admirably designed in their general effect, in which soundness and honesty of construction go hand-in-hand with picturesqueness of style. The two houses on the right of the illustration are peculiarly noticeable. The porches are protected from the street by their guarded approaches, walled in by massive and richly-decorated stone balustrades. In the first example the simply designed oriel-window of the second story is surmounted with vase-like decorations, and makes an open balcony for the third story. The adjoining house is still more striking in architectural character, from the double oriel front and the dormer-windows which project from the attic. Both these houses are somewhat Elizabethan in their style, and succeed in combining the as-

pect of solidity with lightness and grace, a result more easily attained, perhaps, by the judicious use of the oriel and dormer window than through any other means.

A good example of tasteful and attractive fronts may be noticed in Fifty-seventh Street, between Fifth and Madison Avenues. Here the porch does not project, and is entered directly from the street, the only distinguishing feature of the arched doorway being the difference of color in its upper facing. In one of these houses a fine oriel-window, which also furnishes a balcony for the second story, gives a decorative

Façades, Madison Avenue, near Fortieth Street.

effect to the house-front. Dormer-windows in the steep triangular roof, which is laid in bright tiles, give an additional effect of picturesqueness. These houses have a peculiarly bright, open, cheerful look, which attracts the fancy, perhaps, more than would more somber dwellings, far more elaborate in style and decoration.

The new buildings of Columbia College, in Madison Avenue, between Forty-ninth and Fiftieth Streets, are good specimens of the Elizabethan style, and impress the mind pleasantly from the cheerfulness of their aspect. Gothic windows in the first story, square windows above, oriels placed here and there, and dormer-windows in the roof, break up the severity of the front, and give a decorative effect without detracting from the cloister-like air which seems peculiarly suitable to a college structure. Buttresses rising in pillar-forms high above the eaves of the roof subdivide the front, and lessen that uniformity which arises from a long succession of architectural effects similar in character. Some of the newer buildings of Yale and Harvard may be more elaborate in their decorations, but we know of no college structures in America in which simplicity and grace of outline are more appropriately dignified by ornamentation, or better suggest the purpose and nature of the buildings themselves. Columbia College has only for a short time been settled in its new home, but it has just reason to be proud of its success in suiting the structural design of a college, while it has added buildings that dignify and ornament the city.

In Fifty-seventh Street, west of Fifth Avenue, may be admired a residence which has no superior in New York for rich and elaborate but tasteful ornamentation. It begins with that sound principle of taste that

Façades, Fifty-seventh Street, between Fifth and Madison Avenues.

the appearance of solidity and strength should never be sacrificed to the purely decorative element. This is carried out from the foundation to the roof, and nowhere do we see a suggestion of that finical style which sacrifices mass and dignity to the mere art of the stone-cutter. Yet the whole façade presents a variety of ornamental effects, which make the house one of exceptional beauty. The first striking feature which we notice is the triangular oriel, presumably the outlook of the drawing-room, which marks the first story. This projects so far as to furnish a base for the bay-window of an octagonal shape on the front of the second story, which has also a quaint little iron balcony running out flush with the outer projection of the first oriel. Crowning this bay-window is a large and roomy stone balcony, on which the elaborately decorated windows of the third story open. The porch is richly carved, rising in graceful lines to the support of a pretty balcony, which has a fine Gothic window-frame above. Dormer-windows surmounted with finials break the lines of the tiled roof, and complete a very pleasing *ensemble*. The basement of the house is massive, and fully equal to carrying off the richness of architectural treatment, which makes the upper stories so attractive. The heavy balustrade which leads up to the porch is carried out on the pavement in a massive wall foundation surmounted by an iron fence and stopped with stone pillars at the area entrance. In this fine house we have another example of the very effective use of different colored stone.

harmoniously suited to produce a decorative effect, and bringing out the essential beauty of lines in more emphatic degree.

Another house in Fifty-seventh Street, of much simpler style, gives us a good example of a second-story bay-window effectively treated. It may be assented that the section of an octagon is on the whole the most desirable form for a window of this kind, as it is not only more ornamental and symmetrical in appearance, but gives

Façade, Columbia College.

also a more perfect outlook for the occupants, which is the principal reason for being of this style of construction. We shall refer to these features of architecture more at length further on, as they make an important element in domestic architecture in New York, after considering another characteristic of New York houses even more *sui generis*—the porch.

Nowhere in the cities of the world can be found more graceful and charming household porches than those characterizing the best residence streets of New York. A pleasant entrance to a building, whether public or private, is like an agreeable title to a book, or a beautiful face in man or woman, which immediately recommends itself as well as what is behind it.

Whether a stranger walk up Fifth Avenue or pass down Broadway, cross the side streets or linger in the squares, we think, if he be from any part of Europe, he must be impressed by the easy access to all the buildings, indicating peace and security. There is nowhere a trace of a thought in the builder of general violence, such as made the heavily-clamped doors of Italy necessary as a bulwark against turbulence and sudden riot. Our little iron grating before basement windows, found almost solely in New York, bears small comparison with the bars as big as a man's arm, which make every considerable structure in Genoa and Florence look like a fortress, which in fact it is, or was when first erected. Our porches, like our general architecture, have their faults, but they indicate a peaceful condition of society, and are only strong enough to resist the weather or a chance vagrant. Our porches thus express our institutions. The peaceful character of the entrance of our buildings to a thoughtful person has the broadest and deepest significance, but yet it touches little *per se* on the æsthetic taste of the people, except in some of the new styles of porches, which are really architecturally beautiful and decorative.

New York porches are cheerful, and almost without exception afford an idea of hospitality and ease, quite unlike the flat wings resembling the doors of a stable or coach-house, level with the sidewalk, which mark the entrance to every house in Paris, except where heavy iron gates, before an iron fence fifteen or twenty feet high, conceal the edifice buried in thick verdure.

Nothing can be more dismal and forbidding than the little dark doors all over London, very narrow and very low; flat with the level of the house, and only raised two or three steps above the level of the sidewalk. These doorways are so inconspicuous that they merge into the general contour of the dark, soot-colored brick wall, and at night it is only above the door itself that a little half-moon-shaped window, banded by an iron framework to small panes of glass, shows the pale lamp faintly glimmering, or else a lantern over the doorway marks its position.

Such is the impression which London makes upon the stranger, and in nearly every city of Europe it is as a means of defense and repulsion, and not of open-handed or open-hearted

Façade, Fifty-seventh Street, west of Fifth Avenue.

greeting, that the doorway seems to have been conceived.

Of the position of the doorway in the general outline of the building there may be grave question, but its pleasantness, *per se*, is another matter. With the impression fresh in mind of the English, the French, or the Italian prison-like barriers against the world without, expressed by their blind and unsightly entrances, multitudes of New York porches abound in grace and cheerfulness. Passing along one of our well-tenanted streets on a spring morning, the sight of its open outside-door-leaves thrown back, to disclose the plate-glass entrance to the vestibule within, is most gay and cheering. Flower-pots frequently abound here, or trailing vines, lodged upon the flat roof of the stoop above, hang in long pendants of green over the brown architrave of stone. Such is the sight on a warm morning; and a mild evening witnesses the family gathered beneath its roof or scattered in the side balconies. A New York land-owner can afford to set his house a few feet back in his lot for the sake of getting freer breathing-space in a widened street in front, and less noise and dust than a closer proximity to the thoroughfare would give him; and, above all, for the sake of having his handsome out-door little room or *loggia* in his projecting porch.

We shall now give some examples of New York doorways, both in public and private buildings, where the type has been modified in accordance with individual taste, and the main fact of a porch is combined with ideas less trite than are shown in the work of ordinary building contractors.

Nowhere are ingenuity and good taste in this respect better exemplified than in some of the new buildings erected by banks and other corporations down-town. There has been a decided tendency of late years among companies, who have been highly successful in their business operations, to commemorate their business achievements by the erection of magnificent structures, unique in their design as well as lavish in their costliness. Some passing glance at these, before studying further the characteristics of domestic architecture, will be of interest to our readers.

In Wall Street, below Broad, the Queen Insurance Company has erected one of the most noticeable business structures in New York. Stone and marble of different colors have been freely used, and the effect is very rich and agreeable, but not meretricious. The ornament is not frittered away in detail, but carried out with

Porch and Window, Fifty-seventh Street, west of Fifth Avenue.

great breadth, though elaborate in treatment. The conception of massiveness and dignity, which is so essential to any great building devoted to business uses, is thus preserved, while the eye is delighted by broken lines and brilliant though harmonious contrasts of color. The architect of this fine building must have had something of the painter's sense, so successful has he been in preserving genuinely artistic combination of color in the use of material, while keeping in view the purposes of the structure.

Low, broad steps lead to the doorway, the whole construction of which is admirable. The porch is heavy and massive, overhung with a richly decorated Gothic arch. This rests on short pillars, Corinthian in style, of variegated red marble, and the latter are again supported on buttress-like pilasters, carved with the peculiar Corinthian decoration. Pillars resting on but-

Porches in Wall Street, below Broad.

tresses also decorate the window-facings, and carry out the general design. The marked features of this building are the beauty and originality of the porch and the effective use of color in architecture, and, for this reason, single it out as one of the most striking types of the tendencies of architectural art in our midst. The great activity of property-owners in the business portions of New York in tearing down old buildings, many of them still fine structures, for the purpose of erecting new ones, will probably soon decorate the city with many business buildings, no less beautiful in design and treatment than the noble quarters of the Queen Insurance Company.

Another striking example of the decorated porch in the business building may be seen on the corner of Nassau and Beekman Streets. The

mirably as it takes the carver's tools, its liability to flake off, crack, and become disfigured by dirty weather-stains, has always been an objection to it. One may see whole squares of fine buildings in Fifth Avenue and other streets, where the surface of the stone has been so gnawed and honey-combed by time and weather as to present a most unsightly aspect. The Connecticut sandstone, which is the best, has become so expensive on account of the great difficulty of working it, that people erecting houses have been tempted to try other poorer quarries, and the result may be seen in many a disfigured and ugly front.

Many good effects are produced when in English-basement houses a square, projecting porch, wide and deep, rises but a foot or two above the sidewalk, and is made to unite and

Morse Building is built of red, pressed brick, and is remarkable for its elevation and massiveness. Its architectural beauty, however, is principally observable in the treatment of the porch and windows. The round arch of the doorway is surmounted by a triangular pediment, and the elaborately carved buttresses that frame in the porch give great dignity to its general effect. While lingering at this impressive street corner, one is reminded of the fact that brick is coming more and more into vogue again in New York. Fifty years ago this material was the favorite among builders and architects, and justly so on account of its great adaptability for decorative purposes, its richness of color, and its indestructibility. Brown-stone then became the rage, and has since been the most popular material. Beautiful as freestone is in texture, and adform into the main line of the façade, by a small bay-window in the second story extending so as partially to occupy its flat roof. Bay-windows, especially when they extend as sections of an octagon, are among the most graceful and elegant features of house convenience and beauty; and when, as in one of these that we recall, just out of Fifth Avenue, the extension is so shallow as to allow of a little balcony to intervene between its French windows and the projecting top of the porch, its bright-green plants and shining plate-glass windows are pleasant and elegant. The essential point that should be striven for is to place porches quite low in the line of the house-fronts. The slight difference between the elevation of the flight of steps that may be seen in the houses at the corner of Fifth Avenue and Eighteenth Street, and the narrower, higher, steeper ones of their neighbors, will convince most people of the instinctive feeling of agreeableness which one derives from a low-setting porch. With the comparatively great height of New York houses, the proportionate size of the foundation should be commensurate, but in such cases it ought, to have an æsthetic effect, to be apparently concealed, as, for instance, by the broad and broken line of side-steps, for the same reason that we bank up or terrace over the cellar-walls of our homes in the country. The porch of Trinity School, in Twenty-fifth Street, is an excellent example of this arrangement. A good specimen of the opposite of this class of faults is afforded by the excessive size and undue covering up of the lower story of the Academy of Design, whose porch is large enough and whose rising steps are broad enough for a building of double its height and double its size. The illustration we give affords a very good idea of this section of the building. The porch and stairway are fine in themselves, and from the color and detailed ornament of their ma-

terials are still more striking. All who have seen it will remember the very imposing Giant's Staircase which leads from the pavement to the *première étage* of the Ducal Palace at Venice. Large and ponderous in detail, it is yet strictly in keeping with the length and height of a building on whose general style the National Academy was professedly constructed. Our thoughtful architects build for the future, and it was in anticipation of the time when the Academy-wall might be continued to Twenty-fourth Street, and take in a much larger section between Fourth and Madison Avenues, that this doorway, with its high, pointed top, its pleasant marbles, and its careful carvings, was constructed. At present, however, the building seems rather an appendage of the front door, than the latter to afford an opening to an important interior.

Porch of Morse Building, Nassau, corner of Beekman Street.

The porch of the Dry Dock Savings-Bank, which is attached to one of the most interesting buildings in New York, shares with the rest of the structure the advantage of having been planned by a very able and imaginative architect. This is no exception to the rule of the agreeableness of a porch that stands low with the side-wall. Placed at an angle of the Bowery

Entrance to the Academy of Design.

presence, and it is besides very suggestive in its details. In the same way that the minute carvings of ivy-leaves, oaks, and woodbine, are an agreeable study in the pillars and iron railing of the Academy of Design, so the lace-like tracery in the gray sandstone above the arches and above the columns of the porch of the Savings-Bank is highly grateful. In this Moorish-Arabesque work, the taste of the architect, who has made this tracery an attractive feature of the introcessed arched doors of the Jewish temple in Fifth Avenue, is conspicuous.

But while the doors of New York houses form the most numerous class of pleasant, convenient, or cheerful entrances, though mixed with plenty of poor ones, the churches of the city give the best opportunity for the display of the experience and taste of the builder. We have said that, if it were possible, the porch should form a dignified architectural section of each building, which these little square extensions, with their breaking line of steps, do not always fulfill. Every one familiar, either in reality or by photographs, with the great churches of Europe, will recall how often the lofty arch of the main entrance glides in structural effect into the contours of the big, round window above it, whose framework and decorations in their turn form part of the rising lines which end in the pointed front of the majestic edifice. This idea, we think, is the right one, and the doorways of some of our own churches bear out this relation. Many of these, and especially the Gothic ones, have doorways which begin a series of breaks to a receding

which allows the main wall to recede from the street, a corner is formed for this porch, which enables it to project twelve feet or more, and not interfere with the line of the sidewalk. The porch, with a second story added to it, forms a dignified feature of the structure, and it otherwise would be insignificant and trivial if composed only of a little square projection from a long and high façade. Its upper story gives it

wall of a high tower, as may be seen particularly in the two on Fifth Avenue between Fortieth and Fiftieth Streets. The new Catholic Cathedral carries out the intention of the European church-door fully, and its very high, arched entrance, so rich in carved detail and in clustered columns, seems a fitting support, with the heavy pillars that form the sides of the arches, to the great carved-stone window-frame above it.

Of pleasant church-doors, that of the Church of the Heavenly Rest, in Fifth Avenue near Forty-fifth Street, of which we give an illustration, is one of the most elegant; constructed largely of colored marbles, polished and carved, its broad, low, front porch and its rich color make it a conspicuous ornament to the avenue.

The new buildings of the city present most frequently interesting doors, but in some of the oldest structures of New York we find agreeable objects to contemplate. The shallow Grecian porch, which characterizes some of our old-fashioned houses, has been condemned by many, but it has a certain austere cheerfulness of its own not to be overlooked; and strolling along busy Broadway at noon, or after the sun has lengthened the shadows on the tall stores that surround it, the weather-beaten front of St. Paul's is full of pleasant associations, with its brown walls, its white-marble memorial tablets, and the carved bass-reliefs above it, now subdued and softened by time. It has an interest to the antiquarian and the artist that is absent from many a newer structure. Houses, too, not yet very old, have a pleasantness all their own. Open garden lots between Eighteenth and Nineteenth Streets in Fourth Avenue, in the back of which, on either side of the avenue, stand old-fashioned, comfortable dwellings, whose iron balconies make one of the most agreeable features about them, offer a pleasant rustic picture to the eye. Extending across the width of these ample fronts, the verandas with their roofs, and partially covered with iron trellis-work, half veil alike the long French windows which open out upon the balcony, and shield the front door from too curious eyes. The door-steps are quite low and few, and the slight height of the basement is hidden from observation by the extended iron-work and by low shrubs.

The conventional "high stoop," which is found in so many New York houses, is peculiar to the city. In the expensive houses in Fifth Avenue and its cross-streets, the old-fashioned stoop has been modified and elaborated into a roomy and imposing porch, generally supported by Corinthian pillars, the architrave, fringe, and cornice above being of the same style. As this

Porch of Trinity School, Twenty-fifth Street.

stoop is higher than it was in the original from which it is descended, it has a questionable feature in the necessity it involves for a long row of steps rising twelve or fifteen feet to connect the homestead with the outer world. When, however, the steps and balustrade are so arranged as to form an important feature in the lower structure of the wall, it only needs that the front doors should be placed together by pairs, to double the pleasant break in the appearance of

Porch of the Dry Dock Savings-Bank.

the foundation, and to remove the sense of awkwardness and unfitness which one has in surveying the ordinary high stoop.

An excellent example of a doorway with side-steps may be seen in East Thirty-sixth Street. The balustrade facing the street gives a slight sense of privacy, while the top of the projecting roof of the porch forms an up-stairs balcony pleasant in its suggestion as a small sitting room for warm evenings, and is as important in giving dignity and mass to the porch as a heavy Grecian architrave would be. There are a good many varieties of these side-steps in the city. Where we find them in a house on a corner lot, which gives opportunities for pleasantly arranged end-windows, and also in many cases for a little strip of sodded yard to skirt the house, the effect is peculiarly agreeable. In one house of this description, the building does not occupy the entire width of the lot, and the steps and opening in a stone balustrade begin ten or twelve feet to the side of the front porch. Rising from the sidewalk by three or four low steps, a square platform makes an agreeable landing half-way up, and, at right angles to the others, a few more stairs bring the visitor to the broad platform of stone beneath the projecting roof of the front doorway. Such an arrangement, with its turning and its broken line, adds to the sense of space about a dwelling, and, while the reason is aware that the house is really at the usual distance from the sidewalk, fancy cheats the feelings, as it does in the multitude of windings in Central Park, when we believe that we have gone a long distance even where we can see that the path we quitted ten minutes ago is only two or three rods from us. It is said that the hearth and the front door are the strong points of pleasure and pride to every housewife, and it is to be hoped that, with the revival of the open fire, the importance of a cheerful, a beautiful, and an easy entrance to the hospitable home will be generally recognized.

The striking use of towers and windows as a feature of architectural decoration among the newer houses erected in the fashionable streets of

New York can not fail to impress every beholder, some descriptive allusion to which has been previously made. The house on the corner of Fifth Avenue and Fifty-seventh Street, one of the largest and finest in New York, may be cited as a noticeable example. The building itself is of red brick, and, occupying several lots on Fifth Avenue, extends back to the full depth of a lot or more on the side street. It stands immediately opposite the costly Vanderbilt mansion, which has already been described. It is a little withdrawn from the line of the street, and this serves to heighten the effect of its various stories. It is of irregular elevation, and terminates in some portions with large Elizabethan gables, whose pointed roofs cover four tiers of windows from the pavement to the top. Another section of the house is one story high, and is surmounted by a big glass conservatory with a circular roof. The little oriel-window, which projects from the façade on Fifth Avenue, is itself graceful and pretty enough to give elegance to an abode of which it were the sole ornament. Throughout this house its variously grouped windows of different size are enriched by brown freestone copings and ornaments carved in flower or leaf forms, and from its very broad, round-topped front door to some little windows scarcely larger than port-holes in the main wall, it appears as if the architect had exhausted his ingenuity to give variety and piquancy to what looks like an Americanized French château.

The tower which forms the northwestern corner of the dwelling is as picturesque as the oriel-window, and, while its real structure is merely an extension of the ordinary rooms of the house in the section which it covers, its little pointed, round roof gives a variety to an ordinary bay-window vastly more pleasing and impressive from this change of apparent purpose. To the many-varied forms of this tasteful mansion the architect has added massed and stacked chim-

neys, which, usually dotted about in insignificant points on many American houses, are so ugly, but which, used with effect, are so great an ornament, with their broad, flat surfaces adding

Porch of Church of Heavenly Rest, Fifth Avenue, near Forty-fifth Street.

importance to a side-wall, or breaking the monotony of a dull line of roof. Nature herself is more fertile than human art in covering up and converting the baldness of her uses by the pink light on a rain-cloud, or the purple beauty of rocky crags; and the soft haze which rests upon a landscape gives fully as deep a joy as the thought that its moisture is reviving grass or flowers. The satisfaction which is felt in honest structural forms may be carried too far, if, for example, it disdains those trivial graces and slight additions which would convert a recess in an apartment into such an oriel-window as we have placed before our readers, or form a series of such addition into the elegant finish of a graceful tower.

On the north side of Fifty-seventh Street, near Fifth Avenue, stands a house showing a peculiarly effective oriel-window. As there is

8

Old-style Doorways.

a forcible suggestion of home comfort and domestic ease in a roomy porch, so, even where there is no particular architectural effort aimed at, the appearance of a projecting window to

A Fifth Avenue Porch.

the sitting-room, sunny and filled with flower-pots, or of the wide and light children's nursery window, or a little balcony or vine-covered piazza, has a happy or tender suggestion quite different from anything that appeals to the artistic sense or the intellectual appreciation. The bay-window of our illustration is of this class. Built above the door and first-story windows, it makes one of a number of somewhat similar projections extending along the brown-stone line of houses on the north side of this street. Ruskin speaks much of the pict-uresqueness of irregularity; and in such edifices as the Dry Dock Savings-Bank, or the new Court-House in Sixth Avenue at the corner of Tenth Street, the odds and ends of corners, gables, or recesses, are powerful points of effect, designed by the architect. But, outside of this intel-lectual arrangement of forms that appeals directly to the eye and the imagination, there are at present, scat-tered all about the United

States, irregularities in building that are traceable wholly to the needs and conveniences of the people. The need of piazzas, the convenience of bigger rooms, and the tradition of the advantage of sunshine, have led everywhere to ugly or pretty extensions, as the case may be; and such additions cover all classes of buildings, from the little square porch of the day-laborer to such elaborate and costly structures as this carved and variegated bay-window in one of the best rows of New York houses. As indications of the needs of our people, these architectural features are desirable, and by-and-by their forms, not always now pleasing and artistic, will spring naturally from the taste and discrimination of our people, and architects of skill will shape this taste into beauty and symmetry as a rule, just as they have done already in a number of excep-

Porch in Fifth Avenue.

Porch in East Thirty-sixth Street.

tional cases. So American city architecture may be made as appropriate for America as the old palaces of Venice are for Italy. In the mean time we may be thankful for such artistic treatment of the bay-window as we show in several of the illustrations of this book.

A pretty window belongs to a house in Thirty-fourth Street near Fifth Avenue. The house has a narrow front and is four stories high, surrounded by buildings larger than itself. The second story of this dwelling is covered by a deep and wide balcony made of brown-stone, that occupies nearly its entire width; and the third story to which the window in the picture belongs is almost concealed by equally heavy balconies. Here we find an example of the fact that details good in themselves may fail in their object by too great or too little prominence. This window with its accompanying balcony is elegant, with graceful carving, and the window with its cheerful draperies is played on by the sunlight, whose dappled sheen alternately brings into relief the little stone leaves of the ornaments, or the projecting angles, or pillars or balls on the balcony. Yet the effect is greatly lost because the structural form of the house is entirely covered up and lost sight of by the fringes and ruffles of stone drapery that overhang and overlap the corners and the main entrance; and, while one or at most two such bits of decoration as this would give life and vivacity to a house-front, the ornament repeated and piled one above another becomes tedious. The little window that would suggest home-like comfort or cheerful society is shorn of its charm by the thought that it is not a circle of friends or a family group who would enjoy it of a warm evening, or that it is ever the

only fit for the gathering of groups to witness processions, or as the outlet for crowded balls, or they merely show an ostentatious love of display in the owner, or a poor, half-developed taste in the architect.

There is, probably, no question which so taxes the invention of the architect as what he shall make the main feature of one of our narrow city houses, whose owner expects from it a combination of originality and attractiveness. Fortunately for the public, the time for contract-planned houses, each as like the other as pens in a pod, is now largely superseded by designs that at least indicate thought on the part of the man who planned them; and so we see house after house springing into existence, with a peculiar tower on one, a strange ornament on another, or, as in the example of the house in East Thirty-seventh Street, a large gable, that projects only enough to show that it is a gable, relieves the flatness of the general wall, and separates this house as an individual structure from the mass of its neighbors.

This house, which is situated at a short distance from Madison Avenue, is a brick building, covering two lots in its width, the red color of which alternates with a gray freestone in large masses about its lower story. Many of our readers are familiar with the beams, horizontal and transverse, that show the structure at the same time that they compose the decoration of the old gable-ends of roofs in the ancient cities of Europe. Between such beams in Chester in England, in Beauvais in France, as well as in a multitude of similar cities and towns, yellow stucco, broken and moss-grown, yet clings to rough stone or brick walls that compose the edifice. Decayed timber in these beams often presents the picturesque and worm-eaten appearance of age, while the projecting eaves of

Porch, Thirty-ninth Street, east of Park Avenue.

gathering-place for children tired of their nursery. In this multiplicity of balconies all feeling of sociability is destroyed, and such places are

the stone roofs alternately shadow or illumine such ends of houses, when the sunshine lights up the yellow or brown lichens that cover them, or dim- the recessed wall, dreary unless enlivened by the presence of pigeons or swallows. Here in America we have little chance to see these time-worn and time-beautified edifices, unless it be in some old dwelling in a Dutch town of New York State, and, instead of the architectural variety of aspect afforded by the old network-like timbers on these gable-ends, the architect falls back upon such ornament or variety as the materials to his hand afford him. The most convenient and easy method of decoration is reached in America at the present time through the use of variously-colored stone, or of bricks, either in flat vaults, or with their ends fitted edgewise to the angles of the main wall. The architect of the pretty and original façade of the house in Thirty-seventh Street has availed himself of these mural decorations, and we see in the concave-pointed roof, with its one window, several tiers of black bricks, forming a tooth-shaped ornament, and this gable is separated from the story below it by an elaborate row of gray carved

ornament of tesselliated black brickwork, and this story in its turn is marked off by stone-carving. The second floor of the house exhibits one

Oriel-Window—Fifth Avenue and Fifty-seventh Street.

Tower—Fifth Avenue and Fifty-seventh Street.

stones. The next story of the gable, whose front is broken by a group of three windows in the center, is in its turn relieved by another broad

window embellished by the gray-stone balcony that forms at the same time a pretty finish to a bay-window that composes the lower section of this gable. The gable projection occupies rather more than half the width of the house, and is bounded on either side by a narrow, flat wall with one window group in each story, and with a small bay-window in the second story dominating the front door.

In New York, the eye jumps from a Saracenic temple, like the Temple Emanuel in Fifth Avenue, to a Gothic cathedral like St. Patrick's, or to a French château like that at the corner of Fifty-seventh Street and Fifth Avenue. Directly opposite the latter building, on the east

Bay-Window—Fifty-seventh Street, east of Fifth Avenue.

Window—Thirty-fourth Street.

structed very largely in this effective style; and the long rows of such buildings suc-ceeding each other for miles, as one drives toward the Arc de Triomphe or along the Rue de Rivoli, impress the beholder as belonging to a city of palaces.

side of Fifth Avenue, rises a white-marble pile, looking not unlike many of the aristocratic houses of Paris.

The style of this pile, extending from Fifty-sixth to Fifty-seventh street, is very ornate, but, compared with the Corinthian, the Doric, and the Renaissance style of ornament so profusely superimposed upon most of the plain flat blocks of houses all over our city, its propor-tions smooth themselves out into simple masses that please if they do not entirely satisfy the eye. Few residences in New York present such great architectural complete-ness as this series. Extending with a very long front on Fifth Avenue and on the side-street, the building has the mass and the proportions of a public edifice. Its high square corners rise much above the re-maining portion of the roof, and present the effect of massive tow-ers, while the symmetrical disposi-tion of the windows and colonnades increases its appearance of unity. The new houses of Paris which stand upon the boulevards are con-

Gable—East Thirty-seventh Street.

There is, however, a certain tedium in this unending stateliness, this continuous splendor. The little palaces mingled with big ones, with different ornament and varied roofs, that charm the eye and excite the imagination by their unique design in Venice, have always the stimulus of novelty, and have none of the appearance of being turned out by wholesale, or by gigantic machinery, that is so wearisome in avenues like the Boulevard Haussmann. To those who believe that the ideal of such a street as Fifth Avenue would be completed when, by the gradual survival of the fittest, the separated brown-stone houses have all gradually disappeared, to give place to blocks crowned with towers, or where one elegant and varied roof should suffice to

Mansard Roof—Fifth Avenue, corner Fifty-sixth Street.

cover many residences whose proportions have relation to one general effect, such a structure as this would be a model. The white-marble house in Fifth Avenue is of such a character, and, while the divisions and doors that mark it as the house of many families are not at all conspicuous, this stately building is distinct of its kind in the whole length of the avenue.

A pretty and simple specimen of the tower is that of Trinity Church School, which is a not very conspicuous feature of the large brown-stone building seen across the graveyard of Trinity Church. It is a picturesque pile, and reminds one of some English college-building with its multiplicity of Gothic mullioned windows. The tower rises only slightly above the edifice, but its long gargoyles, extending far over the sides, are quite conspicuous even from Broadway. In spite of the insignificance of its situation, it commands attention and interest. As the spectator looks at it from Broadway, crowded with vehicles and foot-passengers, a quiet and picturesque repose lingers about the walls of the secluded building, and its charming, quaint little tower gives a peculiar Old-World appearance to its aspect.

It is pleasant to find in a monotonous line of freestone houses with their Greek porticoes and high stoops the occurrence of an occasional break. The pedestrian, tired by repetition of form in buildings, suddenly, for example, finds his eye refreshed as it lights on such an odd and irregu-

Tower—Trinity School.

the house-front, and quite high up in the air, aims primarily at being a bay-window, and one of its two sides faces obliquely southward, while the opposing angle of the tower looks up Fifth Avenue.. The builder, not contented to give the form necessary for use, has capped the top by a tall and slender pointed roof whose shining brass trimmings add to its picturesqueness, while an elaborate ornament of the same metal, that rises high above the apex of the roof, renders it still more conspicuous.

Close by Park Avenue in Thirty-sixth Street stands a large dwelling which is very tasteful and decorative. It extends the entire depth of the block, and in the extension just beyond the main dwelling is placed the odd and pretty little belvedere, an illustration of which is shown. Many houses, both in city and country, contain conservatories, used partly for plants and partly for sitting-rooms. Here against the shining glass

Turret—Fifth Avenue, near Twenty-second Street.

lar turret as that one we show near Twenty-second Street in Fifth Avenue. It is not alone that such a picturesque object gives us pleasure, but one sympathizes with the poetical or fanciful turn of the builder, and, while the eye is allured by graceful form, the mind is pleased in the consciousness, thus tangibly aroused, that there are others than humdrum Gradgrinds. The little turret whose picture we give is built to cover the third and fourth story middle windows of a large shop. The building is constructed of red brick, and its windows are mostly pointed and united into groups by brown and gray freestone copings, while in spaces between the stories buff and black brick-work is arranged in tessellated designs. The little turret, projecting well beyond

windows stands of flower-pots and tall flowering trees, such as oleanders and pomegranates, alternate with sewing-tables and children's toys, easy-

Belvedere—Thirty-sixth Street near Park Avenue.

chairs and writing-desks, and these sunny parlors furnish an agreeable variety to the ordinary sitting-room or the conventional greenhouse. In a great many parts of Southern Europe the custom of having gardens and terraces upon the house-tops is very common, and many travelers will recollect the tall pots of aloes, the clustering rose-bushes, and the deep-green myrtle trees upon the roof of the Doria Palace, the Pallavicini Palace, and many other of those princely mediæval abodes of Genoa. But as yet, in Northern American cities, we have none of these luxurious hanging-gardens, that are more fitted for tropical than for northern climates, and it is only here and there that some such little nook as the pretty belvedere of our picture gives the suggestion of a real out-of-door garden forming a portion of a house. This belvedere forms a second story open bay-window, unenclosed by glass above its windowed counterpart in the ground-floor. A rounded balcony of gray-stone screens this bit of summer-garden with its flowering

shrubs, or its bed of evergreens; and slender pillars, whose carved capitals support the arches of the roof, are formed of a similar material. Across the top of the long extension of the house a similar balustrade ornaments the roof, while on the side of the main section of the dwelling one or two bay-windows vary the monotonous flatness of the dead-wall. Architectural features of this class give great charm to many streets in the newer parts of the city.

An agreeable and picturesque contrast to the elaborate Buckingham Hotel, at the corner of Fiftieth Street and Fifth Avenue, is made by the modest group of brick and freestone buildings that stand behind it in Fiftieth Street. Opposite the stately white walls of St. Patrick's Cathedral these pretty fronts group themselves

Tower—Fiftieth Street, near Fifth Avenue.

on the south side of the street. The tower forms an addition to the room from which it projects, as shown in the illustration, and the slightness of the means taken to secure so important a result by roofing in this little projection and ornamenting its top by a slight trellis-work of iron and gilt is specially pleasing by showing how good taste will utilize trivial means. The house to which this tower belongs is good in many particulars. Its little bay-window stands well in regard to the tower, and its round-topped windows, grouped in various clusters, afford in connection with the low-porch door, scarcely raised above the level of the sidewalk, a very pleasant, cheery, as well as picturesque bit of house-building.

The last illustration of architectural effects in building which we give shows the tower on the Police Court building at the junction of Sixth Avenue, Tenth Street, and Greenwich Avenue. The tower is as unique as the building to which it belongs, and rises to a considerable height in a circular form, much above the level of the surrounding houses. Its decoration consists chiefly of a spiral line of white stone that winds around the tower, passing between the windows and along the edge of the little loop-holes that light the various stories nearly to the roof. The only fault one can justly find in this tower is the shape of its roof, which, instead of diminishing gradually to a point, as is usual in many objects of similar construction, whose proportions are justly admired, has superimposed upon its solid proportions the inevitable square-sided roof which we have borrowed from the French Mansard, and which, though appropriate in its place, is often ugly when used in connection with incongruous architecture. In other respects the effect is very pleasing. Several other towers even more graceful in shape rise from the roof in just proportion and relation, and stacked chimneys and dormer-windows are used very effectively.

Other examples might readily be cited displaying the unique and interesting features becoming more and more common in the architecture of New York. But enough has been shown to indicate what is unquestionably the fact, that there is springing up among us a style of building which, though composite in character, is picturesque and tasteful.

Tower—New Court-House, Sixth Avenue.

PARKS AND PLEASURE-PLACES.

Central Park

IF there be any point in New York to which more than another there can be attached an enduring memory, it is the attractive and picturesque locality known as Central Park. Twenty-five years ago it was mainly a wild, uncouth domain, the salient objects of which were swamps, bowlders, and huge, knotty projections of rocks forbidding in their aspect, and promising anything but that wonderful development of beauty which has since become manifest under the skill of the engineer, architect, landscape - gardener, and sculptor. Travelers, who have visited probably every famous park in the world, pronounce eulogiums upon this pride of the American metropolis, which leave no room to doubt that, if it is not already, it will eventually become, the most beautiful park on earth. Its trees do not possess the grandeur of age, but its shrubbery has attained a luxuriant beauty not often excelled. Central Park, in its large proportions — embracing as it does some eight hundred and forty-three acres, an area which extends from Fifty-ninth Street to One Hundred and Tenth, and from Fifth Avenue on the east to Eighth Avenue on the west — in its exquisite lakes, where in summer one may sail in fairy-like boats, and almost be lost among the shady nooks and dells where the swans glide peacefully; in its cozy recesses found by devious paths, its artificial caves, its springs of water flowing from rocks that have been tapped by the rods of modern prophets, its suburban views and villas, its luxurious resting-places for the weary, its rural decorations, its grand lawns and extensive drives on roads that are the perfection of art, its various amusements offered to the public for a mere trifle of expenditure, its bridges, restaurants, towers, tunnels, and sculptured works—surely there can be no place in Christendom more calculated to appeal to that taste for and sympathy with Nature which exists in the hearts of us all.

Visit it at any hour of the day, and you will find thousands gathered to enjoy their walks or drives. Music lends its enchantment to the spot in the summer, and in the winter the several lakes are given up to the sports of the skaters and curlers. There is, indeed, no nook or corner in the vast reservation that has not been beautified. And every year witnesses some change, some additional improvement. Hundreds of thousands of dollars are annually expended in this work; and when at last it shall be completed, and it has become a complete treasury of art, science, and natural history, as it now is in part, when the avenues by which it is bounded have been lined with handsome mansions, and grown shadowy with trees, the famed parks of ancient Europe will pale before the beauty and magnificence of that which is even now the admiration of all who see it.

Central Park is essentially a democratic place. It was created for the enjoyment of the people, and, when you drive there on a Saturday or Sunday afternoon, you will see a brilliant and ever-changing pageant, such as you will not find elsewhere. The most expensive vehicles of the wealthy classes will be mingled with the humbler barouche that has been hired for the occasion by a family pleasure-party, or perhaps you may find yourself side by side with the grocery-wagon of some sturdy German who has brought his *frau* and little ones to enjoy the stirring scene, and is *en route* to the lager-bier saloons of the upper portions of the island. Everything, in fact, belongs to the living panorama, from the nurse and baby-wagon to the old-fashioned rock-away of the Westchester farmer, and the landau of the fashionable lady. Fast horses and many of the celebrities of the city are frequent visitors to the park, and perhaps it is the best of all localities in New York wherein to observe the characteristic phases of out-of-door metropolitan life.

Yet one can not see the park to advantage from a carriage-window, but must go on foot. The charm of such a pleasance is not merely in its broad and frequented avenues, but in the thousand nooks and corners, the tortuous windings and turnings, where one continually meets the unexpected and finds himself secluded from all the suggestions of busy life, while the fresh air, the sweet scents of grass and flower, the shaded quiet, and the songs of birds, surround him with all the associations of country life.

Perhaps in no way can we convey a better idea of the multiplicity of attractions in Central Park, which has justly been called the lungs of New York, than by giving a few statistics. The length of carriage ways or drives, ranging from fifty-four to sixty feet in width, is about nine miles; the length of bridle-paths, having an average width of sixteen feet, is a little over five miles; and the footpaths, which are from thirteen to forty feet in width, make a total of more than twenty-eight miles in length. There are thirty buildings of all kinds in the park, and seats to accommodate ten thousand persons, a large number of these seats being in shaded grottoes. On the four hundred acres of grove there have been planted since the opening of the park about half a million of trees, shrubs, and vines, and a large proportion of the former have become noble trees. Exclusive of the reservoirs, there are about forty-three acres of water, divided into six charming lakes and ponds, in several cases these little sheets of water being so winding and irregular that rustic bridges are thrown over them.

Scattered about the park are bronze statues or busts of Burns, Alexander Hamilton, Fitz-Greene Halleck, Humboldt, Mazzini, Webster, Shakespeare, Schiller, Sir Walter Scott, and Morse; and ideal statues symbolizing Commerce, the Indian Hunter, and the American Soldier. The most noble and striking monument in the park, however, is the Egyptian obelisk, known as Cleopatra's Needle, which was recently brought across the seas from Alexandria, Egypt, by Lieutenant-Commander Gorringe, of the United States Navy. Most of the statues in the park have been severely and justly criticised; but, aside from the question of artistic merit, on which the majority of the visitors who go for recreation to Central Park are entirely incompetent to decide, these bronze figures give an air of dignity and public interest to it, which even cynical critics would hardly care to dispense with.

Let us first take a stroll over the Mall, which is the grand promenade, extending about the third of a mile from the Marble Arch to the Terrace, and giving an excellent view of a considerable section of the park. Near the northern end is the music-stand; and on Saturday afternoons, during the summer months, when the band plays, it is almost impassable, except by moving with the crowd. Sunday is, however, the great gala-day, for then the poor and many of the middle classes of the city throng the park in such numbers that every avenue and winding path is full of people, bent on enjoyment. The Mall is arched over with splendid elms, and along this avenue are ranged most of the bronze statues of which we have spoken. A pleasant feature is the sight of the children in the goat-carriages, from mere babies to well-grown youngsters, who enter into the enjoyment of the scene with more zest even than their elders.

The Mall, Central Park.

At the northern end of the Mall, leading down to the Esplanade on the shore of the lake and containing the beautiful Bethesda fountain, is the principal architectural feature of the park, known as the Terrace. It is constructed of a fine, soft stone of a yellowish-brown color, and the central stairway goes down under the road, where the visitor enters an arched-roofed hall, used as a restaurant. On the side-stairs are beautifully-chiseled carvings of birds, fruits, and flowers wrought on the panels of the wall and along the base of the balustrade. The whole façade of this fine specimen of park architecture is an admirable work, and has been widely and justly admired.

The Ramble is one of the most charming portions of the park, consisting of a labyrinth of narrow winding paths, abounding in delightful bits of scenery, consisting of deep thickets, small streams, and rustic bridges. In this region is the Cave, a deep, rocky dell, where a solemn conclave of owls generally sit in state, and glare at intruders with big eyes. Near the entrance at Sixty-fourth Street, on the Fifth Avenue side, is the Menagerie, which has its quarters in the Old Arsenal, a castellated brick building. There are good in-door and out-door collections of wild animals—lions, tigers, panthers, wolves, bears, monkeys, squirrels, opossums, kangaroos, ostriches, sea-lions, camels, and a hundred curious birds and beasts. This zoölogical exhibition, however, is larger in the winter than in the summer, as in the former season many traveling shows go into winter quarters here.

In the Museum of Natural History, situated between Seventy-seventh and Eighty-first Streets and Eighth and Ninth Avenues, are some very fine collections of rare birds, animals, and insects. In the aggregate, this museum is one of the largest and finest in the country. It also contains a meteorological and astronomical observatory, and a gallery of art. One of the greatest attractions of the park is the Metropolitan Museum of Art, which is situated on the Fifth Avenue side, opposite Eighty-third Street. The portion erected, which is only one of a projected series of buildings, is two hundred and eighteen feet long and ninety-five broad, and is a handsome structure of red brick, with sandstone trimmings, in the Gothic style. The most important feature of this Museum is the Di Cesnola collection of ancient art objects, exhumed in Cyprus, regarded by archaeologists as the most remarkable of its kind in the world. There are also a number of loan collections of pottery, paintings, sculpture, arms, wood-carvings, etc.,

which amply reward the curiosity of the student. The picture-gallery belonging to the Museum contains some of the best examples of the old Dutch, Flemish, and Spanish masters to be found in America. This Museum stands within a few feet of the East Drive.

There is no attraction in Central Park which will be gazed on with more curiosity and interest than the obelisk which was presented to the city of New York by Ismaïl Pasha, late Khedive of Egypt, and brought across the ocean through the remarkable engineering skill of Lieutenant-Commander Gorringe, United States Navy. It stands on a knoll in the grounds adjoining the Metropolitan Museum, and occupies, as it deserves, one of the most commanding situations in the park. This monolith carries us back to a period more than fifteen centuries before Christ, and it is probable that Moses gazed at it, even then many generations old, while he was a priest at the city of On, or Heliopolis. According to the hieroglyphical writings inscribed on its side, it was made at the order of Thothmes III, one of the greatest conquerors among the Egyptian kings, who carried his arms among all the nations of the East, to commemorate his victories. This is one of two obelisks erected at the city of the sun-god, Heliopolis, by this monarch. Three centuries after his death, vacant spaces on this monolith were inscribed by order of Rameses II, who appears to have been the Greek Sesostris, and also a great conqueror, with records of the latter's achievements. Under the Greek dominion of the Ptolemies, this wonderful monument of the most ancient civilization in the world was removed from its time-honored site at the city of On to Alexandria, where it occupied a place which made it almost the first object greeting the eye of the voyager on entering the harbor. When Augustus Cæsar and Mark Antony fought their tremendous duel under the very eyes of the beautiful Cleopatra, this was already nearly fifteen hundred years old, and it looked down unchanged on all the warlike convulsions, "the drums and tramplings of conquest after conquest," which have swept over Egypt in successive waves. Of the different Egyptian monuments which have been removed from their native land and erected in foreign countries, including those in Rome, Paris, and London, the New York obelisk, known as Cleopatra's Needle, is the most remarkable and historically interesting, as well as the most perfect in its preservation. The bystander who can look at this dumb but eloquent witness of nearly thirty-five centuries of the world's changes and catastrophes without a strange thrill must be, indeed, callous and lacking in imagination.

A charming place for a ramble or drive may be found in Riverside Park, a narrow and irregular strip of land lying between Riverside Avenue and the Hudson River from Seventy-second Street to One Hundred and Thirtieth Street. Between the western limit and the river, however, passes the road-bed of the Hudson River Railway. The general width of the park is about five hundred feet, while its entire length is some three miles, the area being about one hundred and seventy-eight acres, only a portion of which has been laid out in walks and drives, while the rest still retains the wild picturesqueness of nature. The surroundings of this park are so lovely that it is believed it will ultimately become the most aristocratic residence region of New York. The ground rises to a bold bluff above the Hudson River, and the views from the river driveway are very charming, giving glimpses of the

Terrace, Central Park.

Central Park Drive

wavelets, and the Wee-hawken heights oppo-site. Within its limits is the Claremont man-sion, named after Lord Clare, a royal colonial governor; and perched at the bifurcation of two large oak-limbs is a marble bust of George II, which was brought to this country by a Dutch ship, and ante-dates the famous one which once stood on the Battery.

A famous resort in connection with the turf interests of New York is the race course known as Jerome Park, which was laid out and beautified with trees, shrubbery, a club-house and other necessary buildings, by Leonard W. Jerome. Turf amusements n u m b e r among their patrons many of the most wealthy and influential residents of the city. The American Jockey Club, organized in 1866, leases Jerome Park, and it is under their au-spices that the most ex-citing races run in the vicinity of New York are conducted. This park is situated near Fordham, in the ex-treme northern suburb of the city. The track is an excellent one, and on a knoll in the cen-ter stands the club-house, which is a hand-some and well-appoint-ed structure, containing parlors, large and small d i n i n g - rooms, and sleeping- and retiring-rooms. The house is surrounded by a wide veranda, and the lawn is terraced down to the track. On racing-days

undulating, tree-covered park, the shining stretches of the river dimpled into innumerable these are covered with ladies in bright toilets, and the drags of the Coaching Club are drawn up near by. Opposite the club house are the large grand stand, the quarter-stretch (where the betting men congregate), the judges' stand, etc. The American Jockey Club is really the most prominent racing association in the United States, numbering as it does some fifteen hundred members, and including representatives of nearly every wealthy family in the city. It is presided over by Mr. August Belmont. The Club gives two meetings annually, one early in June and the other early in October, during which there are five, six, and sometimes seven days of racing. Horse-racing has not become so essentially a national pastime in America as in England, and nowhere in this country do we ever see such a scene of enthusiasm and interest as that of Derby Day on the Epsom Downs of England, which so engages the attention of all classes as to supersede all other interests whether of business or pleasure. But a racing-day at Jerome Park, if it can not boast of the universality of interest and that picturesqueness which comes of an immense throng of all classes meeting for the nonce on terms of democratic equality, has a gayety and attraction of its own which make a visit on one of these occasions an agreeable episode.

The most unique and attractive pleasure resort in the vicinity of New York is found, however, at Coney Island, only a few years ago a barren waste of sand, with a few low taverns, given over to the amusements of rowdies and "demi-reps," but now crowded with magnificent hotels and all those attractions which make the seaside delightful for a day's visit. Of its kind there is no watering-place in the world which has so many individual fascinations as Coney Island under its present *régime*.

Coney Island is the extreme western end of a great outlying sand-bar broken by inlets, extending along the coast of Long Island for ninety miles, other sections being known as Rockaway, Long, Jones, Oak Island, and Great South Beaches. Coney Island is a part of the town of Gravesend, and is separated from the shore by Gravesend Bay on the west, Sheepshead Bay and Coney Island Creek on the north. On the east it runs out to a sharp point, and has the broad Atlantic for its southern boundary. Its distance in a bee-line from the battery to the wharf at the western end of the island is eight and one half miles. Previous to 1875 this fine stretch of sea-beach, with its splendid surf-bathing and its convenient location with reference to access from New York and Brooklyn, was a mere waste of barren sand except at the west end of the island, where there was a small hotel, to which two steamboats made daily trips, and at the terminus of the Coney Island road, where stood another wretched hostelry,

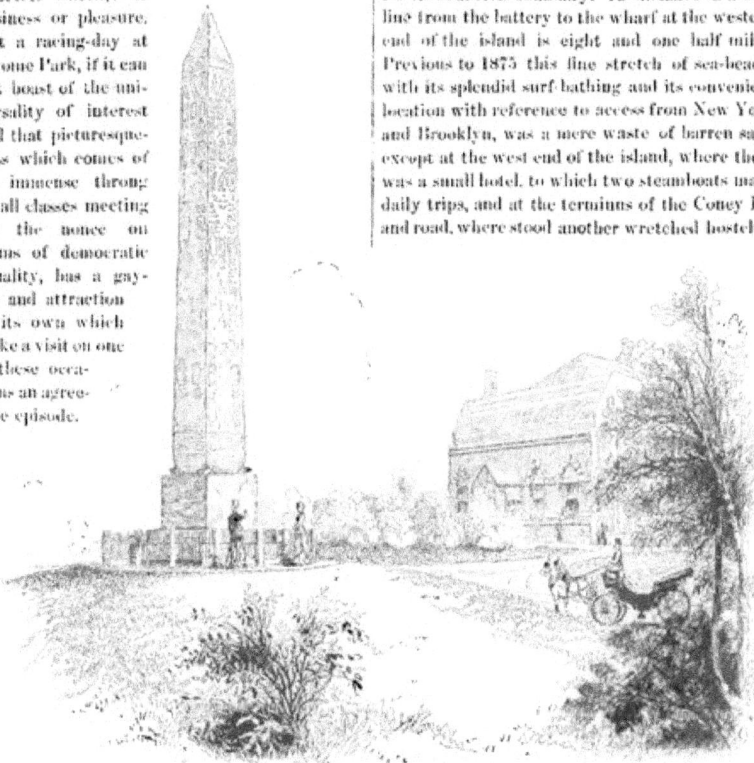

The Obelisk, Central Park.

to which driving parties from Brooklyn sometimes came. But the beach, as has been previously indicated, was but little visited by the more refined classes, its wonderful facilities for sea-bathing and enjoyment of the fresh ocean-breezes being for the most part given up to the rough and dissolute, who were wont to turn the beautiful beach into a pandemonium. A single horse-car line from Fulton Ferry and a steam line from a remote portion of Brooklyn, near Greenwood Cemetery, furnished the means of reaching the other portions of the beach. In 1874 a steam road from Twentieth street, Brooklyn, was built by an enterprising capitalist to what is now known as West Brighton Beach, and a large pavilion and restaurant were erected at its terminus. The result proved that the enterprise necessary to afford a convenient means of reaching the island was all that was necessary to secure for the place the position to which its location and natural advantages entitled it, as the most popular watering-place in this country. At the present time eight steam-railways, one line of street-cars, and nine lines of steamboats, capable of transporting at least one hundred and fifty thousand persons to and from the beach daily, are in operation. The beach itself is covered with light and airy buildings of all sizes and for every conceivable purpose, and during the season the sands are black with people daily. Three of the hotels are among the finest of their kind in the world, and a number of others are fully equal to the best hotels at other watering-places. The island is now divided into four parts, known as the West End or Norton's Point, West Brighton or Cable's, Brighton Beach, and Manhattan Beach. Beginning at the West End, or Norton's, the island has been but little improved. The beach is covered with the refuse thrown up by the tides, and the surface of the island is covered with irregular hummocks of fine white sand and an occasional growth of beach-grass and laurel. Norton's Hotel is an old, low, wooden building, back from the shore, and a wooden path leads down to a large pavilion. Accommodations are provided here for parties with lunch-baskets, and there are numerous unattractive-looking bathing-houses. Between Norton's Hotel and West Brighton Beach there are fourteen small hotels and pavilions. The principal hotel at West Brighton is known as Cable's, and this point is about the center of the beach. The scene here is suggestive of a huge fair-ground. There is a broad plaza in the center, with green grass and flowers, traversed with wide modern pavements. Besides Cable's,

there are several other very decent hotels clustered about the plaza. Every afternoon and evening a band plays at the pavilion near by, and the scene at night is illuminated by the brilliant rays of the electric light. A camera-obscura gives excellent views of the beach, which are well worth seeing; and an observatory, three hundred feet high, the top of which is reached by large elevators, affords a splendid outlook over the island, the bay, and the adjacent cities.

One of the most striking features of this part of the island is the pier, one thousand feet long, built of tubular iron piles, which runs out a thousand feet into the sea. On it are three two-story buildings containing saloons, restaurants, and promenades, twelve hundred bath-rooms, and stairways leading down into the water from the pier. Steamboats from New York land at this pier nearly every hour all day.

A wide drive and promenade about half a mile long lead to Brighton Beach on the east. Park wagons are continually passing to and fro to convey those too tired or too lazy to walk. From a point about half-way between the two latter-named beaches, an elevated railway will run to Locust Grove, connecting there with steamboats from New York. Brighton Beach is one of the pleasantest parts of the island, and is a favorite resort of Brooklyn people. If it is a little less gay and showy in its surroundings, its air of home-like comfort in the appointments of its buildings will more than compensate in the opinion of many people. The hotel is an ornamental wooden structure, five hundred and twenty-five feet long, and three stories in height, with broad piazzas extending around the whole building. From every one of its towers during the summer season streams bunting, as is the case with all of the buildings on the island. The hotel is handsomely finished and decorated, and in its furniture and appointments will compare favorably with most city hotels. Twenty thousand persons can be easily fed here during the day. In front of the hotel an orchestra of sixty performers play during the afternoon and evening, and the grounds are prettily laid out with walks, grass, and flowers.

From Brighton Beach the grounds of Manhattan Beach extend eastward for two miles and a half. The hotel is a fine wooden building, six hundred and sixty feet long, and three and four stories in height, said to be one of the largest structures of the kind in the world. It is richly furnished and admirably appointed in every particular, the permanent guests having sole claim to the use of the upper floors, while the lower floors and

Riverside Park.

marine railway runs westward to the Brighton Beach Hotel, along the sands; and a new road will soon be built on piles across Sheepshead Bay to the racecourse of the Coney Island Jockey Club. Music is furnished, as at the other principal hotels, from the pavilion in front, and an immense throng may be always seen here, listening to the music, which is of the finest, chatting, laughing, flirting, and otherwise enjoying a delightful open-air concert with its enlivening and joyous surroundings. Four thousand persons can dine at one time, and thirty thousand during the day. In a grand pavilion near the hotel fifteen hundred persons can sit at table. Visitors who bring their own lunch are provided for here, and capital dinners of sea-food can be had. The bathing-houses to the left contain twenty-seven hundred separate rooms, and the arrangements are perfect in every respect. The beach in front is fenced in, and the inclosed space rigidly reserved for bathers. Large floats beyond the breakers afford resting and diving places for expert swimmers, and life-boats patrol the beach at the same point. The ladies' bathing-houses are separate, and hot and cold salt-water baths in private rooms are provided for those who do not

piazzas are given over to the daily visitors. In the rear of the building is the railway-station; a like surf-bathing. An amphitheatre seating two thousand persons overlooks the bathing-grounds, and a band plays here during the afternoon and evening.

East of the Manhattan Hotel is the Oriental Hotel, built by the Manhattan Beach Company, for the accommodation of permanent guests and families who desire to be free from the confusion attending the coming and going of transient visitors and excursionists. It is a picturesque structure six and seven stories high, four hundred and seventy-eight feet long, and ornamented with eight large circular towers rising forty feet above the roof, each surmounted by a minaret fifteen feet high. There are four hundred and eighty sleeping-rooms, handsomely furnished, and the main dining-room is one hundred and sixty by sixty-four feet; and the servants' rooms and the various offices are in the detached buildings in the rear.

From the foregoing description it may be readily gathered that Coney Island is a most remarkable and unique watering-place. Within an hour's journey of New York, it furnishes thousands of people, who can not leave the city during the summer months except for a very brief period, a chance for seaside diversion, bathing, and fresh air, while every resource known which can gratify the most epicurean tastes offers its seductions for the more fastidious public. Indeed, many families, previously in the habit of going for the summer to more distant points, have of late adopted Coney Island for their summer home. It is, however, from the great throng of daily pleasure-seekers, made up of all classes, that Coney Island gains its peculiar picturesqueness and animation. The whole length of the beach on a bright summer day is a never-ending procession of people, from men and women of the highest social rank and position, to humble mechanics and laborers out for a day's airing with their families; and the contrasts of life and character resulting from this heterogeneous assembly give Coney Island its greatest charm, aside from the sea, air, and sunlight.

Coney Island as it was.

Scenes at Coney Island.

THE IRON PIER

Scenes at Coney Island.

BROOKLYN.

Ferry-House, Brooklyn.

A DAY might be well spent by the visitor in rambling about the city of Brooklyn, which contains many objects of local and historic significance, to say nothing of the pleasant drives that abound in its suburbs. The third city in the United States in respect of population, it is essentially a portion of New York, and probably the day will come when it will be nominally as well as really incorporated into the great American metropolis. The "City of Churches," as Brooklyn is often called, is practically a great dormitory or suburb of New York. But little business is done there except what is directly connected with the shipping interests of the port of New York, or such supply-trade as may be necessary for local needs.

Instantly the stranger sets foot in Brooklyn, he is struck with the provinciality and serenity of the place; contrasting so vividly with the feverish energy which makes every pulse of life just across the East River throb so fiercely, Brooklyn in many respects reminds one of Philadelphia in this quiet and peaceful feeling which is diffused through all its associations, and causes one to liken it to a huge, overgrown country village. In some respects, however,

Brooklyn has supplementary advantages which cause it to be of the greatest advantage to New York, aside from its value as a residence region for those engaged in the tumult and hurly-burly of business in the imperial center of American civilization.

Originally settled by the Dutch, like New York itself, the spirit of the old Flemish burgher has impressed itself on the life and traditions of the city with a conservatism which has been still more fed by the fact that a large proportion of the people who have drifted thither come from the Eastern States, and have brought those notions with them which are the outcome of the old New England Puritanism, a power still strong in its essence, though it has passed away as a name.

The circuit of Brooklyn measures twenty-three and a half miles, and the city embraces an area of thirteen thousand three hundred and thirty-seven acres. Its extreme length from north to south is about seven and three quarter miles, and its greatest breadth five miles, the western boundary affording about eight and a half miles of water-front. Williamsburgh, formerly a separate city, was united with Brooklyn in 1835, and is known as the Eastern District. In fact, the city embraces several districts, still locally known by the names which they bore when they were distinct municipalities. The city has many advantages as a place of residence. It is for the most part considerably elevated

City Hall, with Kings County Court House and Municipal Building in the rear

above tide-water, and is open on all sides to land and sea breezes, while the wide streets, generally at right angles to each other, afford a free circulation of air.

Of the numerous ferries which connect Brooklyn with New York, Fulton Ferry is by far the most important, and is an avenue of travel and traffic whose extent astonishes one when he examines its statistics. Not less than twenty-five million people cross this ferry annually, not to speak of the enormous amount of freight borne on these sluggish, turtle-shaped boats, which play so important a part in the economy of New York life. The ferry-house on the Brooklyn side is a roomy and ornate structure, and there was a time when the most important business interests of Brooklyn were concentrated in its immediate vicinity, but the business center has now shifted to the City Hall, where are situated most of the monetary institutions, such as banks, insurance companies, etc. The great commercial interests lie along the river-front. It is here that Brooklyn plays a most important part in filling a great need for New York ocean-commerce. Brooklyn's extended water-front is completely occupied by piers, slips, warehouses, boat and ship yards, ferries, etc. Here are some of the most commodious and extensive wharves and warehouses in the United States. The immense quantities of grain received here make Brooklyn one of the greatest grain depots in the world. Grain is brought from the Western States by canal and river to the port of New York, and then stored in the Brooklyn warehouses for distribution through the United States and Europe. It is estimated that twenty-five thousand vessels exclusive of canal-boats and lighters are annually unloaded on the Brooklyn side of the East River, and that the total value of the merchandise stores is but little less than three hundred million dollars annually.

One of the most striking features of the Brooklyn water-front is the massive Atlantic Dock, which belongs to a company organized in 1840, and the first to provide extensive ship accommodations of this kind. This fronts Governor's Island, near the south extremity of the shore-line, and is a basin in the form of a parallelogram, with an area of forty acres, and a depth of twenty-five feet, being sufficient to float the biggest ships, five hundred of which can find quarters in it at once. The Brooklyn Basin, the Erie Basin, the Wallabout Basin, and others, also furnish equally extensive facilities for the accommodation of vessels and the commerce of which they are the indispensable vehicles. It will be easily admitted, then, that the Brooklyn water-front, with its incomparable accommodations for shipping, is a necessary supplement to New York and the interests of the port.

About a half-mile from the Fulton Ferry stands the City Hall, at the junction of Fulton, Court, and Joralemon Streets. This is a fine structure of white marble in the Ionic style, with six columns supporting the roof of the portico. Its dimensions are one hundred and sixty-two feet by one hundred and two, and seventy-five feet in height, comprising three stories and a basement; it is surmounted by a tower, the top of which is one hundred and fifty-three feet from the ground, and which contains a clock, the dials of which are illuminated at night. This building was erected in 1845, at an expense of two hundred thousand dollars, though the original plan, which proposed a much greater structure, would have cost more than five times that amount.

The Kings County Court-House, which is situated on Joralemon Street, in the rear of the City Hall, extends back to Livingston Street and fronts on Fulton Street. It is one hundred and forty feet wide and three hundred and fifteen feet in depth. The height is sixty-four feet, and the building is surmounted by a cupola composed of ribs and panel-work of iron, rising one hundred and four feet above the ground. The main edifice is constructed of Westchester marble, in the Corinthian style of architecture, and it was erected in 1862, at a cost of five hundred and forty-three thousand dollars. Adjoining the Court-House, as shown in the illustration, may

Academy of Music and Academy of Design.

be seen the Municipal Building, also on Joralemon Street. It is a fine structure of marble,
with spacious rooms and hallways, and is occupied as the headquarters of the police and for
other municipal purposes. Near by this vicinity,
in Washington Park, are interred the remains of
the ill-fated prisoners of war who died on the
terrible prison-ships, and were first buried on
the adjacent shores of the Wallabout. After
some years of agitation, the bones were finally

collected in 1808, and laid in a vault near the
Navy-Yard with imposing ceremonies. In 1873
they were transferred to a vault constructed
for the purpose in Washington Park (old Fort
Greene), where it is also proposed to erect a
monument to the memory of the martyrs.

Other imposing buildings are the County Jail,
in Raymond Street, a heavy-looking, castellated
Gothic edifice of red sandstone; the Penitentiary,
in Nostrand Avenue, near the city limits; the

Long Island Historical Society Building.

State Arsenal, in Portland Avenue near Washington Park; and the City Hospital, which stands
on elevated ground in Raymond Street near De
Kalb Avenue. This building has a front of two
hundred feet, and consists of a main building,
four stories high, fifty-two feet in width and
depth, with a rear extension of thirty feet; and
two wings, each seventy-four feet long, fifty-six
feet deep, and three stories in height.

On Montague Street, west of the City Hall,
may be observed two fine structures devoted to
the fine arts, the Academies of Music and Design, both of which are admirably fitted for
their purposes. The Academy of Music is the
property of a stock company, and was erected in
1860, at an expense of two hundred thousand

dollars. It is constructed of brick, with Dorches-
ter-stone trimmings, and has a front length of
two hundred and thirty-six feet, with a width of
ninety-two feet in the rear. The interior is richly decorated in dark colors, and the seating capacity is twenty-three hundred. The opera companies which have given performances in New
York have always appeared in this opera-house
of the sister city, so that Brooklyn has heard for
a number of years simultaneously with New
York all the great singers who have come hith-
er from Europe. The Academy of Design adjoins the Academy of Music, and is a highly
ornamental structure of the southern Gothic
style of architecture, built of brown sandstone.
It has one small and two large rooms for the

Brooklyn Scenes—Clinton Avenue; Clinton Street; On the Heights.

exhibition of pictures, lighted from the roof. It communicates with the second floor of the Academy of Music by large doors. The Brooklyn Art Association holds two annual exhibitions of pictures here, in the spring and fall. On the opening night there is always a full-dress reception, when the Academy of Music is also thrown open. Admission can only be obtained by card from a member. The pictures are mainly loaned by wealthy connoisseurs and by artists; and the work of the scholars in the principal Brooklyn schools is also exhibited. After the opening, the pictures remain for two weeks on free exhibition. Many of the finest pictures which are exhibited

Prospect Park.

first in the New York Academy of Design also find their way into the Brooklyn exhibitions, so that the latter are but little less attractive than those held in New York as representative of the best art of the time.

Another important institution, which is the outcome of the intellectual needs of the time, is the Long Island Historical Society, which occupies a fine large brick structure, seventy-five by one hundred feet in size, with terra-cotta and stone trimmings, at the corner of Clinton and Pierpont Streets, adjoining Trinity Church, which was completed in the spring of 1880. There are a fine hall, a library containing twenty-six thousand volumes, an equal number of pamphlets, and a museum with many curious relics among its treasures. Persons not residents of Brooklyn are admitted on the introduction of

a member. This society has already played a
highly important part in the collection of old
colonial records and other national antiquities.

Brooklyn is celebrated for its churches, and
contains some of the foremost preaching talent
of the country. Plymouth Church, where Rev.
Henry Ward Beecher is pastor, is one of the
most celebrated institutions of its kind in the
United States, and is a great attraction for both
strangers and residents. The church is a huge
brick building of great architectural simplicity,

containing the largest church-organ in America,
and having a seating capacity of twenty-eight
hundred people. The building is generally
thronged to hear the famous pulpit orator, and
one may easily find the way thither by merely
following the crowd. It is said that the income
of the church merely from the sale of pews is
nearly seventy thousand dollars a year. Other
well-known Brooklyn churches are St. Ann's
(Episcopal), at the corner of Clinton and Livingston Streets, of the middle pointed Gothic style,

Greenwood Cemetery.

built at a cost of two hundred thousand dollars; the Church of the Holy Trinity (Episcopal), which has a spire two hundred and seventy-five feet high, and is generally of great architectural beauty, at the corner of Clinton and Montague Streets; St. Paul's (Episcopal), at the corner of Clinton and Carroll Streets, a handsome Gothic structure, which cost one hundred and fifty thousand dollars; the "Church of the Pilgrims," where Rev. Dr. Storrs is pastor, a noble edifice of gray-stone with a commanding spire, at the corner of Henry and Remsen Streets, which contains in the wall of the main tower a piece of the "Plymouth Rock" on which the Pilgrims disembarked; and the Tabernacle, in Schermerhorn Street, a square, brick amphitheatre, said to be the largest Protestant Church in America, where the Rev. T. De Witt Talmage, one of the most sensational preachers of the time, holds forth weekly. The Roman Catholic Cathedral, which is to occupy the entire block bounded by Greene, Lafayette, Vanderbilt, and Clermont Avenues, when completed, will be one of the largest and finest church edifices in the United States, if the full design is carried out.

The most attractive and aristocratic portion of the city is known as Brooklyn Heights, so called from its commanding altitude, from the top of which may be had a fine outlook over New York Bay and City. The streets crossing this elevated part of Brooklyn are lined with handsome residences, which vie with the costly structures of Fifth Avenue and its intersecting streets, and here dwell many of the prominent business and professional men of New York. Clinton Street, on the "Heights," is lined with beautiful residences, and is the fashionable promenade, where on a pleasant afternoon or evening may be seen much of the wealth and fashion of the city. Columbia Street, which reaches the most elevated height in Brooklyn, just at the approaches of the Wall Street Ferry, is also a charming promenade, and contains many fine mansions. The most attractive street, however, is Clinton Avenue, which is of great width, ornamented with splendid shade-trees, and lined with beautiful residences, surrounded by extensive and highly embellished grounds. In the latter respect, Clinton Avenue surpasses anything which can be found in New York. Our illustration gives a view of Columbia Street on the "Heights," Clinton Street, and Clinton Avenue, which may be considered among the finest residence thoroughfares of Brooklyn. Among other fine streets are Bedford Avenue, containing several large churches, New York and Brooklyn

Avenues, and St. Mark's Place, where there are many striking residences in the French château style.

The "City of Churches" has very appropriately the most beautiful and extensive cemetery in the city of New York, and one of the most beautiful in the world. Greenwood, as this great necropolis is descriptively called, forms a tract of nearly one mile square, comprising four hundred and fifty acres, and lying about two and a half miles from Hamilton Ferry in the southern portion of the city. It is reached by numerous lines of cars, and at all seasons of the year, but particularly during the summer, when its undulating surface is covered with verdure, it will be found a very picturesque and lovely spot. Greenwood Cemetery is managed by trustees as a public trust, and the fund for the improvement and permanent care of the grounds amounts to six hundred thousand dollars. This cemetery was formally opened in 1842, and since that time there have been nearly two hundred thousand interments. Many of the lots are held at a thousand dollars each.

The northern entrance buildings are of great architectural beauty. The recesses above the gateways are filled with groups of sculpture representing in front our Saviour's entombment, and the raising of the widow's son; on the reverse or inside may be seen the carved representation of the raising of Lazarus, and the Divine Resurrection. It does not lie within our limits to do more than hastily notice the costly and beautiful monuments, which so thickly strew the natural loveliness of grass, tree, and lake, improved by the art of the landscape-gardener into the most exquisite combinations. Among these memorials may be mentioned the following: The John Matthews monument, which was erected at an expense of thirty thousand dollars; the monument and bronze bust of Horace Greeley, erected by the printers of the country; the Brown Brothers monument, erected to commemorate the loss of six members of the families of the great bankers on the Arctic; the Firemen's monument; the chapel monument to Miss Mary Dancer; the marble temple of Scribner and Niblo; the Charlotte Canda monument; the Soldiers' monument, erected by the city of New York to those soldiers who had lost their lives in the late civil war; the James Gordon Bennett statuary group; the colossal bronze statue of De Witt Clinton; and the Louis Bonard monument. All these mementoes of the dead are of great beauty and lavish costliness, and are only a few of the remarkable mortuary memorials to be seen by the visitor, who may easily spend a day in an interesting ramble through the cemetery.

An afternoon may also be delightfully spent in driving through Prospect Park. With just pride the people of Brooklyn claim that this great breathing-spot surpasses in natural advantages its older rival across the river, and there are certainly features of forest and plain, of hill and dale, of rolling ground and extent of scenery, which with the unbiased visitor go far to justify the boast. The work of laying out the park was not begun until the month of June, 1866, and the progress made is surprising. The ground was purchased at an outlay of four million dollars, and the total cost, including improvements, has been about nine million.

The area of ground within its limits covers five hundred and ten acres. The principal entrance, on Flatbush Avenue, know as the Plaza, is paved with Belgian pavement, and ornamented with a fine fountain and statue of the late President Lincoln, and is bordered by grassy mounds decorated with shrubbery. The drives extend over a distance of eight miles, besides which there are three and a half miles of bridle-road.

The pathways and rambles for pedestrians are lined with trees, and amply supplied with drinking-fountains, arbors, and rustic shelters. The lake covers an area of sixty-one acres, all of which are in winter allotted for skating.

The highest point, Lookout Carriage Concourse, is seven eighths of an acre in area, and is a hundred and eighty-six feet above the ocean-level. The view from its summit on a clear day is wonderfully beautiful. Thence can be seen the Highlands of Nevisink, Staten Island, the Kill van Kull, hills of Orange, the Palisades, etc. Elegant resorts are scattered through the park, furnishing simple and wholesome refreshments for visitors. A grand boulevard has been opened from the park to the ocean, two hundred and ten feet wide, and six and a half miles long, making perhaps the most delightful drive in the vicinity of New York. At the southern end of the park is a parade-ground of twenty-five acres used by the National Guard of the two cities for semi-annual inspections, and at other times for polo, cricket, base-ball, and other manly games. On Saturday afternoons a fine band plays in the park, and attracts many additional visitors.

Bird's-eye View of Atlantic Docks, Brooklyn.

OTHER POINTS OF INTEREST.

DECKER BROTHERS' PIANOS.—WHERE THEY ARE MADE.

ONE of the busy establishments of New York City is the Manufactory of the celebrated Piano-forte makers, Messrs. Decker Brothers, whose instruments have attained a world-wide reputation. Here, under the personal supervision of the founders of the house, the vast detail of all that appertains to the manufacture of a perfect instrument goes on. Their buildings are situated at Thirty-fifth Street and Eighth Avenue, and are well worthy a visit of those who are interested in witnessing the many and varied processes by which this instrument is produced.

The foundation of the house of Decker Brothers was unostentatiously laid in 1862, with a small capital in money, but a capital large in experience in all that was necessary to produce instruments to sell to a critical public—experience gained by an acquaintance from their earliest youth with every (even the minutest) detail of the mechanism of the piano-forte, and by having filled the most responsible positions in the establishments of the earlier manufacturers of our time. They indulged in no rosy fancies of sudden popularity and a quickly-realized fortune. Of simple tastes, they undertook the business not so much as a means to wealth as for the purpose of improving the manufacture. Being practical artisans themselves, and familiar with the capabilities of every man employed in the business in New York, they found no difficulty in securing the services of the highest skill for each department. Good mechanics prefer employment where their ability is not only well paid for, but is also properly appreciated, and the estimation in which the Decker Brothers were held was such as to cause the leading journeymen in other factories to seek engagements at their hands.

The instruments manufactured by this firm fully realize the standard of what a well-made piano, for tone and durability, should be. The firm is one of the most prominent of representative piano-forte makers in the world, having won this proud position by the intrinsic merits of the instruments of i s make.

Their warerooms, at 33 Union Square, is also a pleasant place to visit. Here will be found many superb specimens of artistic skill in this direction, both as to musical excellence and exquisite exterior ornamentation and finish. Strangers, even if not intending to purchase, but who wish to examine, will be welcomed, and afforded every opportunity for testing the tone and for the inspection of the finish of their pianos. The location of the building is convenient, being on the most prominent thoroughfare in the city.

We give illustrations of the stores of Messrs. A. T. Stewart & Co. on other pages in the body of this work, where they are but just mentioned as we pass along up Broadway. But here we give a more extended account of these most wonderful establishments, not to gratify the curiosity of New-Yorkers, for there is probably not one who does not know all about them thoroughly; but in answer to the inquiries of the stranger—for none ever come to our city but they seek out and visit "Stewart's." The building, located on Broadway and Chambers Street, is six stories in height, overlooking the City Hall Park, and runs from Chambers to Reade Streets, extending back on those streets some three hundred feet. When erected, this great block of marble was considered to be "up town," and twenty years ago it was as fashionable for ladies to shop there as it is now in Stewart's grander temple of trade on Broadway, Ninth to Tenth Streets. It is constructed of the purest Westchester marble, and in the Corinthian order of architecture, and its appearance to-day is as fresh and pleasing as when first opened to the public nearly thirty years ago. Within this period many other styles and orders of architecture have been tried and adopted in the construction of business-edifices in our city; but, among them all, none appear more beautiful or better adapted to the taste or the wants of the immense business, to accommodate which it was erected. Until recently this building was completely devoted to the wholesale department of their immense business; but the offices have now been moved to the larger building above. Immense as the stock displayed is, it forms only a small part of the whole, as compared to the mass of goods on storage at the various public stores in this city, Jersey City, Brooklyn, and elsewhere, many of which are wholly filled with the property of this firm.

The retail establishment of Messrs. A. T. Stewart & Co. (see page 66) occupies the entire square of ground contained within Broadway, Fourth Avenue, and Ninth and Tenth Streets, covering an area of over two acres, and is, with its seven stories, containing over sixteen acres, devoted alone to the retail trade of this gigantic concern. This building is the first and only one of its kind in the world constructed wholly of iron, standing alone, unsupported by any surrounding walls. It is an enduring monument to the mind that conceived it and to the architect who executed it. With no obstructions to the eye, upon entering, the visitor has before him, at one glance, the two acres of floor upon which he stands. Here, as in the wholesale department, order is the first rule. No unseemly haste or bustle is allowed, but everything is quiet and business-like. No more beautiful sight can be had in New York City on a pleasant day than can be obtained by a visit to this establishment. On the first, second, and third floors, are exhibited the finest productions of Europe and America; while, looking down from the dome upon the vast multitude of ladies and customers usually trading within these acres of space, a view is to be had the like of which can be found nowhere else, either in this country or Europe.

W. H. SCHIEFFELIN & CO'S, CORNER WILLIAM AND BEEKMAN STREETS.

W. H. Schieffelin & Co.'s large and well-known drug house, in William Street, is in one of the most active business centres in the city. Their establishment is the oldest and most extensive in the country; it was originated before the beginning of the present century, and has now the confidence of a vast constituency, extending through all parts of the Union. This vast warehouse, through all its numerous stories, is crowded with goods in every department of their multifarious business, and the stir and bustle of their immense trade would interest and surprise the stranger.

LIFE INSURANCE.

LIFE INSURANCE, though hardly known in this country thirty-five years ago, has grown to be one of its most important financial interests, and one which has a direct bearing upon the welfare of thousands of women and children at a critical period of their lives. We have selected as a representative of this interest the NEW YORK LIFE INSURANCE COMPANY, one of the old *purely mutuals*, whose history covers nearly the whole period of the life-insurance business in this country, and whose age, prosperity, honorable dealings, and present standing, combine to make it representative of the best features of American Life Insurance.

The COMPANY'S HOME OFFICE, 346 and 348 Broadway, New York (an illustration of which we give on page 19 of this work), was erected by the Company in 1868-'70. The ground dimensions are sixty feet front on Broadway, one hundred and ninety-six feet on Leonard Street, seventy-one feet wide in the rear, and one hundred and ninety-seven feet on Catharine Lane. This site, being centrally located, is one of the most valuable in the city, and has long been a favorite one with New-Yorkers. It was formerly occupied by the Society Library.

The building presents an imposing exterior. It is built of pure white marble, in the Ionic style, the design having been taken from the Temple of Erectheus at Athens. The portico at the principal entrance is twenty feet in width, projects four feet from the main building, and has double columns on each side. Upon these rests a cornice, with a broken pediment, in which is set, in sculptured marble, the insignia of the Company, viz., an eagle's nest, and an eagle feeding her young. The coat-of-arms of New York City appropriately crowns the front of the edifice. The roof is of iron, and the building is fire-proof throughout.

The interior of the building is in keeping with its general character—simple, elegant, and perfectly adapted to the purpose for which it was erected. The offices of the Company are at the end of the hall, on the first floor. The main room takes in the whole width of the building, and is one hundred and ten feet long through its centre. Side-rooms at the rear end serve as offices for the President and Vice-President, Medical Examiners, and Directors, and as fire and burglar proof vaults for the securities and books of the Company. Agents of the Company occupy a part of the second floor, and the remainder of the building is rented for stores and offices.

The substantial character of the building, its great beauty, and its perfect adaptation to the purpose for which it was constructed, combine to make it symbolical of the financial soundness and honorable dealing of the Company, and of that complete adaptability to the wants of the age which has ever characterized its systems of insurance.

This Company completed its thirty-sixth year December 31, 1880. At that time its history and condition were, in brief, and in round numbers, as follows:

History, 1845-1880.

Number of Policies Issued	149,000
Premium Receipts	$91,000,000
Death-Claims Paid	22,000,000
Dividends and Returned Premiums Paid	30,000,000
Payments to Policy-holders plus Assets	90,000,000
Excess over Premium Receipts	8,000,000

Business, 1880.

New Policies Issued	7,000
Amount Insured	$22,000,000
Total Income	8,964,000
Interest Receipts	2,317,000
Death Claims Paid	1,731,000
Dividends and Returned Premiums Paid	2,000,000

Condition, December 31, 1880.

Number of Policies in Force	48,500
Total Amount Insured	$155,000,000
Cash Assets	43,000,000
* Surplus, Company's Standard	4,200,000
" N. Y. State " over	9,200,000

Progress, etc., 1880.

Increase in Assets	$4,186,000
" Surplus, at 4 per cent	2,000,000
" Interest Receipts	281,000
" Premium	643,000
Interest exceeded Death-Claims	586,000

The NEW YORK LIFE has always maintained a deservedly high reputation for careful management, and for liberal dealing with policy-holders. Its great success has largely reduced the actual cost of insurance to its policy-holders, among whom all the profits of the business are divided, and it continues under the same judicious management that has made it a representative of the life-insurance business.

The conditions of a life policy are simple; the payments are small, compared with the indemnity promised; and, if one has a policy in a good company, its ultimate payment may be regarded as sure. There are very many persons who can pay twenty, fifty, or a hundred dollars a year in life-insurance premiums, and never feel the poorer for the outlay, who would save themselves many anxious thoughts, and perhaps save their families many privations and humiliations, by thus investing a part of their surplus earnings. The great recommendation of the system is, that the indemnity it furnishes *begins at once to the full amount of the policy*, as soon as the first payment is made. Thus, for example, the family of a man who insures for $5,000, and pays, say the yearly premiums of $150, is entitled to $5,000 at his death, whenever that occurs. If he lives long, future payments are no great burden, because annual dividends are declared, to be used in reduction of cash payments when so ordered, and when he dies, be that early or late in life, the insurance is a great blessing.

* Exclusive of the amount ($1,752,165.82) specially reserved as a *contingent* liability to Tontine Dividend Fund.

D. Appleton & Co.'s Publishing Establishment, 1, 3, & 5 Bond Street, New York.

APPLETONS' GUIDE-BOOKS.

APPLETONS' EUROPEAN GUIDE-BOOK.

Containing Maps of the Various Political Divisions, and Plans of the Principal Cities. Being a Complete Guide to the Continent of Europe, Egypt, Algeria, and the Holy Land. Completely revised and corrected each Season. In two volumes, morocco, gilt edges, $5.00.

APPLETONS' GENERAL GUIDE to the UNITED STATES and CANADA.

Revised each Season. In three separate forms:

ONE VOLUME COMPLETE, pocket-book form, $2.50.
NEW ENGLAND AND MIDDLE STATES AND CANADA. One volume, cloth, $1.25.
SOUTHERN AND WESTERN STATES. One volume, cloth, $1.25.

With numerous Maps and Illustrations.

APPLETONS' DICTIONARY OF NEW YORK AND VICINITY.

Fully revised each Season. With Maps of New York and Vicinity. Paper, 30 cents.

APPLETONS' HAND-BOOK OF SUMMER RESORTS.

Revised each Season to date. Illustrated, and with Maps. Large 12mo, paper cover, 50 cents.

APPLETONS' RAILWAY GUIDE.

Containing Maps and Time-tables of the Railways of the United States and Dominion of Canada. *Published Monthly.* 25 cents.

D. APPLETON & CO., Publishers, 1, 3, & 5 Bond Street, New York.